The Spirit Set Me Free

The Spirit Set Me Free

True Stories of Faith by Prisoners

Frederick A. Hermann

Paulist Press
New York/Mahwah, N.J.

Unless otherwise noted, formal scripture quotations outlined herein are from the New Revised Standard Version Bible, copyright © 1989 by the Division of Christian Education of the National Council of Churches of Christ in the U.S.A. Used by permission. Scripture in the individual testimonies may be taken, remembered, or paraphrased from a variety of sources.

Cover design by Trudi Gershenov
Book design by Lynn Else

Library of Congress Cataloging-in-Publication Data

Hermann, Frederick A.
   The Spirit set me free : true stories of faith by prisoners / Frederick A. Hermann.
      p. cm.
   ISBN 0-8091-4287-2 (alk. paper)
   1. Prisoners—Religious life. I. Title.

BV4595.H47 2004
248.2'4—dc22

2004013313

Published by Paulist Press
997 Macarthur Boulevard
Mahwah, New Jersey 07430

www.paulistpress.com

Printed and bound in the
United States of America

Contents

Acknowledgments   viii
How This Book Came to Be   ix
Introduction   xi
1. I Had It All   3
2. Now I Know Who I Am   4
3. I'm Up One Day and Down the Next   5
4. Give Me Your Heart   8
5. Everything's Gonna Be All Right   10
6. Everything Already *Is* All Right!   11
7. Come Toward the Light   12
8. I Got a New Heart   14
9. I'm Praying for You!   16
10. Crucifixion in Cell 8   18
11. I Helped Him, Now He Helps Me   19
12. Be with Me in Paradise   20
13. A Weapon to Resist Temptation   21
14. I Had to Lose It All   22
15. I Thought They Were All Fools   26
16. I Found a New Best Friend   27
17. How to Show God's Love   28
18. Those Who Sin Against Us   30
19. I Wanted a Godly Man   31
20. If Someone Hurt You, That Was Me   34
21. I Killed My Wife   36
22. If You Can Do This, So Can I   37
23. Lift Up My Head   42
24. God Cleaned Me   47

25. Let Go and Let God   49
26. God Restored My Joy   51
27. Journey's End   53
28. Is This God or What?   57
29. For the First Time in My Life   61
30. My Past Does Not Dictate My Future   63
31. Locked Up Don't Mean Locked Out   65
32. I Was Headed to Destruction   68
33. From Masks to Miracles   69
34. In This Cell I Am Free   74
35. I've Been Redeemed   76
36. I Thought Christians Were Weak   76
37. Spiritual Warfare   78
38. I Was Blind But Now I See   82
39. I Want Answers   84
40. Prison Taught Me   86
41. Blessed Life, Not Cursed   86
42. I Have Already Received   87
43. Heaven on Earth   88
44. Lack of Knowledge Has Been My Downfall   91
45. It Doesn't Feel Like Prison Anymore   92
46. When I Get Out, I'm Going Right Back In   93
47. I Quit   94
48. I Found Love   95
49. I Found Power and Love   97
50. I Was Hard-Core   99
51. Bring Me an Ax   100
52. Better Off in Prison   101
53. I Was Not Lost But Found   103
54. I've Been Transformed   105
55. I Am at Peace with Myself   107
Prayer Section:
    I Will Trust in the Lord   113
    If These Walls Talked   113
    Praise the Lord   115

Amazing Grace   116
Joseph and the Warden   117
The Lord Is My Shepherd   117
The Beatitudes   118
Teach Me, Jesus   119
Consider It Nothing But Joy   120
Make Me a Captive, Lord   121
The Lord's Prayer   122

Acknowledgments

I dedicate this book to the men and women in jail and prison all over the world.

I give special thanks to my parents for their encouragement. My father declared that he was proud of me for tackling this book. My mother said it would be a blessing to everyone who reads it. She made me promise to write it.

I also wish to acknowledge the following people. Without them this book would not have been possible:

Patty Abel

John O. Dozier

Julie O'Neill Hickey

Kairos Prison Ministry International
(in thirty-three states and five countries)

Kolbe House Prison Ministry Chicago

Paulist National Catholic Evangelization Association
(PNCEA) Prison Ministry (in all fifity states)

Dave Perko

Ja and Arlene Silva, Discipleship Training

St. Louis Police Academy

Rev. James Veltrie, SJ

How This Book Came to Be

One day many years ago, I walked down a dusty road and found myself in prison.

I was on the north coast of the island of Haiti, one of the poorest but most beautiful countries on the planet. I was there as a missionary to teach children how to play soccer, but on this day I journeyed to visit some unfortunate men in prison.

I was led into a cell, and the guard shut the rusty iron door behind me with a clang.

As my eyes adjusted to the darkness, I saw before me six men, all crammed into one tiny cinderblock cell. No electricity, no water. A rusty metal bunk bed leaned against one wall. A filthy bucket, which they used as a toilet, sat on the floor in the corner. The air was putrid, hot, and suffocating.

I introduced myself and soon discovered that most of them had been there for several years. Yet despite these miserable circumstances, they were smiling. I asked how this was possible. One of the men reached back into the gloom and brought forth a tattered Bible. He began to read out loud, "The LORD is my shepherd…"

I was amazed. Here before me stood a man who was truly living his faith, no less than St. Paul when he was imprisoned nearly two-thousand years ago. This one man had effectively shared his faith with his cellmates, and it showed on all their faces.

I had expected to minister to them, but instead they ministered to me.

Upon my return to the United States, I became a volunteer in a local prison ministry, and I led simple prayer services once a week. As the years passed, I heard many heartfelt testimonies from men and women who had discovered their faith in jail or prison. They inspired me to write this book, and these true stories are theirs.

Frederick A. Hermann
Saint Louis, Missouri

Introduction

The first time I heard a prisoner say it, I was surprised, and I shook my head in disbelief.

As time passed, I began to listen more carefully, and it dawned on me that other people were saying the same thing. Not everyone, mind you. Just the joyful ones. At first I doubted their honesty. But gradually I came to realize that many people were indeed sincere. Each was saying, *"Prison is the best thing that ever happened to me!"*

In the pages of this book you will meet these joyful people. They express themselves beautifully. You will hear them describe in their own words how they discovered, to their delight, what they most wanted, in a place where they least expected it.

They are not happy as the world defines it; rather, they are content in a deeper sense. They are peaceful deep down.

Each of them has, as one declares, "looked up."

This explains why most individuals invited me to use their real names. They are not proud of their past lives, but they are no longer ashamed. Because they see their lives in a new light, they are eager to shine this light, to help others find their way. Still, I have changed all their names and references to people and places to ensure their anonymity and guarantee confidentiality.

As you read their stories, you may find that you recognize a part of yourself in each of them. Do not be surprised. Most men and women share similar hopes and dreams, trials and tribulations, sorrows and joys.

You may also begin to realize that *we are all in prison,* in one way or another. Sometimes the people who seem to have it all, those with the most money and the most freedom, are actually the most imprisoned and the most desperately hopeless.

Prisons come in all shapes and sizes. Some people are in a prison made of bricks and steel bars. Some people are in a prison shaped like a whisky bottle, a beer can, a syringe, a casino, or a cigarette. Some people are imprisoned by their lust, or anger, or greed, or jealousy, or worry, or pride.

Whatever separates us from our rightful relationship with our heavenly Father, that is what keeps us in prison, and it is beneath us.

Once we realize this and "look up," we are astonished to see that our Father longs to embrace us in His loving arms. We are overwhelmed by the realization that He wants not to condemn us but to give us life and to give it to us more abundantly.

All of a sudden, we are free to surrender and discover who we really are: beloved children, each one of us, a new creation. Finally we are free to rejoice, to soar above our earthly circumstances, and to join with the psalmist in exclaiming, "Sing to the LORD a new song; sing to the LORD, all the earth."

The LORD *sets prisoners free.*

(Psalm 146)

1.

I Had It All

Dear Friends,

I had it all for a long time. Or so I thought. I wanted the things of this world, and I sure got them all right. Lots of cash, a nice apartment, nice clothes, a good job, as many women and parties as I wanted.

Then I started losing these things, one by one. It hurt. Things I had worked for—I deserved them, they were mine! They were being taken away from me. The more things were taken away from me, the angrier I got.

When I got busted and sentenced to jail, that's when I hit bottom. I finally realized what a mess I had made of my life. A total mess. That's when it really hit me. Then a strange thing happened. I realized that when you're all the way down, you can't go down any more. The only way you can go is *up*. I imagined that I was flat on my back at the bottom of a deep hole, looking up. And you know what I saw? The sky. It was pitch dark, but the stars were twinkling. I started feeling very peaceful, like a lot of burdens had been taken off my back. All those things of the world I had, I saw they were just getting between me and God, separating me from God.

The amazing thing is, when I realized that He was allowing all those things to be taken away from me, and it hurt, I saw that it was because He loved me and didn't want anything to keep us apart. When I understood that, He didn't have to take anything else away from me. I started saying, "Lord, you don't have to take

3

these things away from me any more. I want to give them up for You!"

Ever since, I have been giving my bad habits up on my own. And you know what? The more I give them up to Him, the more peaceful I feel.

J.S.

"Peace I leave with you; my peace I give to you.
I do not give to you as the world gives.
Do not let your hearts be troubled,
and do not let them be afraid."
(John 14:27)

2.

Now I Know Who I Am

I never thought I was a criminal.

And I didn't think I would end up in jail. But I did. I thought my life was over. I hated myself for what I had done.

In jail I found a Bible in the library. My mother had tried to tell me to go straight all the time I was growing up. But I did not listen.

I opened the Bible and looked at it in disgust. It was worn and marked up, and pages had been torn out by other people. I wanted to kill myself.

Then these words from the Bible just jumped out at me, that the Lord punishes everyone He accepts as a son. I almost fell out of bed. That was me, I thought, *me,* these words are for *me.* I don't know how, but it fits me exactly.

I fell on my knees just like a child. It hit me, these words were for me. Now I know who I am. I am a son, and my father God loves me.

J.B.

"My child, do not regard lightly the discipline
of the LORD, *or lose heart when you are punished by*
him; for the LORD *disciplines those whom he loves,*
and chastises every child whom he accepts."
Endure trials for the sake of discipline.
God is treating you as children; for what child
is there whom a parent does not discipline?
(Hebrews 12:5–7)

3.

I'm Up One Day
and Down the Next

I would like you to please pray for me.

I think I have head-knowledge but very little understanding. Sometimes I think I am lazy, other times too overanxious. I would love to just experience ongoing joy, peace, and victory in serving God but I haven't arrived. I'm up one day and down the next.

I think that at this stage in my life there are a couple things that I need to develop. One is hearing the voice of God and knowing without a doubt that it is the Holy Spirit counseling, correcting, and guiding me. I just can't seem to know His voice. I haven't seen or heard from my mom or daughter for awhile, but if they were to speak, I believe I could discern their voices clearly. I also feel I spend too much time doing other things rather than really getting grounded in study and prayer. But I think overall I need to learn God's voice and obey Him.

I pray and I know that I need a personal experience with Jesus and the Holy Spirit. Continue to keep me in your prayers that my faith fail not.

God bless you always, C.J.

For he is our God, and we are the people
of his pasture, and the sheep of his hand.
O that today you would listen to his voice!
(Psalm 95:7)

Do not fear, for you will not be ashamed; do not be discouraged, for you will not suffer disgrace; for you will forget the shame of your youth.

(Isaiah 54:4)

4.

Give Me Your Heart

The jury deliberated overnight, and I was found guilty.

"Oh God! This can't be happening to me!"

I was sentenced to twelve years in prison. The courtroom turned white and my body went numb. I heard the cries from family members behind me as the cuffs were placed on me and I was led from the courtroom to a cell in the basement of the Federal Building.

Sitting on the cold concrete in my business suit, cuffed and shackled, numb and in a complete daze, I realized the war wasn't mine anymore. I needed to let God defeat evil. But where does one start? One doesn't, God does. He went to work the minute I accepted Jesus Christ as my Lord and Savior. This is something I would have never have done in the free world.

From that moment on, the Potter went to work on the block that He had "on order" since the day I was born. Carefully taking the dry clay out of the hard, brittle plastic it was contained in, His hands picked up my shattered pieces that had chipped off from the bumpy delivery ride and began the process more intensely than ever before. I was ready to be molded; it was time for me to come to the water.

It wasn't and isn't an easy process, on either of our parts. I had been broken down little by little. First indictment, then trial after trial, stress, disbelief, incarceration. I was separated from my son and family, my son was forced to go live with his father, my parents were denied visitation, and I realized that the majority of my friends were not really friends at all. And the one simple fact: the situation was out of the hands of myself and anybody I had ever relied on. Mommy and Daddy could not write a note to the warden and excuse me for the remainder of my sentence.

This was something that I was going to have to go through myself. I finally realized there was only one place to turn now, wholeheartedly—*up*. I had been backed into a corner and my eyes could only focus upward. "Oh God!" I prayed. I didn't have the words to pray for myself, only feelings, but I knew what I needed to do because He told me, "Give me your heart." And I did.

The games began. It took me awhile to get used to God as my new coach, and the daily warm-up drills and sprints were challenging. I developed a trust in Him, and He always reassured me that I was doing a good job. If I put my all into my game, I will receive even more back, and I always do. I have learned that it is so much easier just to give it to God and pray. I stand back and watch the wonders of His awesome work. He works it all out for the good, and I trust and believe that. I am willing to accept His solutions because I know that He loves me.

I have learned to praise Him for the good and what I see as bad. I continue to praise Him through my heartache and tears, buckled over, feeling like I want to pass out. I know that this is all happening for a reason and that God has His hands all over my son and the situation.

Our God is protecting all of us because we are His treasures. And when He is ready, in His time, not mine, I will understand. And everything that was meant for evil is going to be worked out for good. And I will that He will bless those that bless me and curse those who curse me; and then justice will be done. Until then, I will sit still and listen. My steps are guided and I am never alone. Neither is my son, and neither are you. I have found the true meaning of "the truth shall set you free." I found it next to the water, where it was all along.

Thank you for your interest in my story. May God bless you.

J.M.

When the righteous cry for help, the LORD *hears,
and rescues them from all their troubles. The* LORD *is
near to the brokenhearted, and saves the crushed in
spirit. Many are the afflictions of the righteous,
but the* LORD *rescues them from them all.*
(Psalm 34:17–19)

5.

Everything's Gonna Be All Right

I grew up bad. Man, I was bad. I knew I was bad, and I didn't even care. I did so many things I can't even remember them all. Tell you what, I should be dead. That's right.

I ended up here in prison, twenty years. I deserve it. I was one of the toughest guys in prison. No one messed with me.

Then one day I saw another guy, a tough guy, too. I saw him walk up to a little guy, who was new and scared, and he said; "Everything's gonna be all right." That's all he said, then he walked on. But it helped that little guy, I could see. I could see it in his face. He settled down. Got confidence. Got courage. And I thought, I'm all torn up inside. Nobody knows it, but that's me too. It helped me to hear that man say it even though he didn't say it to me. There was a confidence in his voice, and he gave his confidence to that little guy. He didn't know it, but he also gave it to me. And I probably needed it more that that other man. I went to a Bible study in our prison block later and found out that the tough guy was a Christian. He opened his Bible and showed me this: "Therefore encourage one another and build up each other as indeed you are doing" (1 Thess 5:11).

Yesterday a new guy was sent to our block. He had the hangdog look, you know, and I passed him and looked him in the eye, and I said, "Don't worry, brother. Everything's gonna be all right. The Lord's looking out for you."

A.R.

O LORD, you will hear the desire of the meek;
you will strengthen their heart, you will incline your
ear to do justice for the orphan and the oppressed.
(Psalm 10:17–18)

6.

Everything Already *Is* All Right!

My stepfather called me when he found out I was in prison. He said, "Son, I'm so sorry; I hope everything turns out all right…"

I said, "Everything already *is* all right!"

I really mean it—God has touched my heart and shown me that He is taking care of me and that as long as I keep following Him, He will make everything turn out fine in the end. But He is also making everything work out fine *right now*.

H.S.

We know that all things work together
for good for those who love God, who are
called according to his purpose.
(Romans 8:28)

7.

Come Toward the Light

Dear Friend,

Hello, how are you doing? I hope and pray you're in the best of health and spirit. As for me, I'm doing just great, having a little family problem, but nothing that our Lord Jesus Christ can't handle. I know He's being a great mediator for me in prison to God the Father. I'm writing because I saw your request for real testimonies of the power of the Lord.

I'm hoping that my testimony can help change somebody's life. It's not my testimony that's going to change their life; it's the power of the one and only Jesus Christ. I'm just hoping that my real-life testimony will draw them closer to the Spirit.

I want to help in any way I can to tell my brothers and sisters about what the Lord has done for me.

Love, D.K.

He himself was not the light,
but he came to testify to the light.
(John 1:8)

*...it is a very small thing that
I should be judged by you
or by any human court.
I do not even judge myself....
It is the Lord who judges me.*

(1 Corinthians 4:3)

8.

I Got A New Heart

Hello, brothers and sisters. I hope and pray that you are all in the best of God's health and spirit. My main concern for writing you is that I am hoping my testimony will give you all hope and faith in our Lord Jesus Christ.

I am very young in my walk with Christ. I am going to share what our Lord has done for me, not because I did good works, but because I was a sinner.

I was in the world robbing and shooting people, and went to prison three times, so when I got out I was a three-time loser. I had a plan. I boxed in prison, and boxing was my childhood dream. I wanted to be champ of the world. So I boxed and worked and stayed clean for five months.

But I started back drinking, and that led me into robbery again. I was going all over doing home invasions, businesses, clubs, a bank, and bars. I also committed a murder during one of these robberies.

Then I was doing a home invasion on a dope house, and someone shot me in the back of the head from about four inches away. My homeboy got me out and to the hospital. I could not walk. Because of the Lord Jesus Christ, I stayed alive. They couldn't take the bullet out because it was near my spinal column in my head. I went through all kinds of pain, and I had to learn to walk again. But because of the Lord's mercy and love, I was whole in no time. But I didn't take this as a wake-up call.

I was back robbing, this time with a grudge. I got in a car chase with the police, and it ended with a shootout. I was shot again in the head on the left side with a .357 Magnum. I was airlifted to the hospital and had brain surgery to remove the bullet. But because of the Lord Jesus Christ's love and mercy, I was saved. I went back to prison on charges of carjacking, attempted murder of a sheriff, and wearing a bulletproof vest while committing a felony. It was on TV and in all the newspapers. My family had to go through this again. I don't remember anything except that it was really, really, really ugly.

This is when the Lord Jesus Christ came into my life to stay, not because I was scared but because He was calling me alone. I have made up my mind and heart to serve our Lord Jesus Christ no matter what the situation may be. I have surrendered my life to our Lord God. It's not easy walking this walk, but you have to let Him have control because the flesh is weak, but the Spirit is willing.

Brothers and sisters, I hope that my testimony has given you the faith you need to trust our Lord's promises because He can't and won't lie. I'll be in prison for the rest of my life, but I'm making the best of it. I challenge all of you to give your heart *all* the way to the Lord. It's a great joy to know our Lord God dwells in you. Jesus is the best thing that ever happened to me. I'm filled with joy and peace, while everybody else who's not in the Body of Christ is down and blue.

I joined the choir. I never thought I'd be singing in church, but that's what the Lord will do for you. The Lord changed my heart from hard to soft and humble. I stay in His word daily; God is good all the time!

Love, F.M.

A new heart I will give you, and a new spirit
I will put within you; and I will remove from your
body the heart of stone and give you a heart of flesh.
(Ezekiel 36:26)

9.

I'm Praying for You!

I was in federal prison for eight years. My own little cell. That gave me plenty of time to think.

Now I'm here in the work release center for a year before I get out. There are a hundred and twenty lost souls packed into four rooms called "dorms" with metal bunk beds and common showers. The noise and smell is enough to drive a man crazy. People yelling and screaming at each other, cursing and swearing all the time. It's like hell.

I started going to a prayer service after dinner on Monday nights, just to get away from the noise.

When the head guard announced the meetings on the loudspeaker and I walked up to the locked dorm door to wait for it to be unlocked, the other guys who were watching TV called me every name in the book. They laughed and called me, "Weak!" "Boy-Toy!" and "Crazy!" They threw soda cans at me as I left. I was scared and didn't know what to say, just hung my head and tried to pretend I was invisible. But I still went, just to get out.

The man who gave this prayer service was not part of the system; he was a volunteer from a local church. I wondered to myself why a man would come here to this hellhole if he didn't have to—he could stay home with his wife and kids.

We talked about how God is real, even if we don't believe in Him. The Lord is real, the man said, and He loves each one of us. I never saw anybody who loved me in my life, that's for sure.

We read the Bible, and I listened, and it was all just words to me, didn't mean nothing.

When the prayer service was over, I'd go back to my dorm, and all the guys would shout and curse the same things. Mean as hell. But I was glad for the peace and quiet.

After a while, I started looking forward to the prayer service. I didn't care what anyone said, I liked it. It was peaceful, the other men who came from the other dorms were like me—they liked a little peace and quiet—and I noticed they were real men.

One night at a prayer service we read in the Bible that we should bless our enemies and pray for our enemies, just like Jesus did. Then we will be like Jesus, sons of God.

It made me think that when those Romans hammered nails into Jesus on the cross, Jesus prayed for them. He said, "Forgive them, for they know not what they do."

Made me realize that Jesus was praying for me even when I was doing the wrong thing.

That night, when I returned to my dorm and a guy shouted at me, I immediately pointed at him and smiled and said, "I'm praying for you, brother!" You should have seen the look on his face.

Now whenever anyone puts me down for going to a prayer service, I say the same thing to them, and it works.

They know I mean it.

L.W.

*"You have heard that it was said, 'You shall love your
neighbor and hate your enemy.' But I say to you,
Love your enemies and pray for those who persecute
you, so that you may be children of your Father
in heaven; for he makes his sun rise on the evil
and on the good, and sends rain on the
righteous and on the unrighteous."*
(Matthew 5:43–45)

10.

Crucifixion in Cell 8

Sometime around the year 1930, no one knows exactly when, something remarkable happened in Cell 8.

It was an ordinary cell with a steel bunk in the central district of the St. Louis Police Department. They use it to hold the homeless overnight, the unfortunate, and the forgotten street people.

A janitor is said to have noticed a man kneeling, as if in prayer, against the back wall. Later the janitor returned and found an empty cell, for the man had been released. To his astonishment, the janitor saw there on the wall a most extraordinary drawing. He beheld a marvelous work, barely visible in the dim light, of Christ on the cross, nearly life-size.

He quickly contacted the officers in charge, who then contacted their superiors, and all agreed that the artist should be located. The search reached throughout the city, then to Chicago and Detroit, then nationwide by the national media. But the man could not be found.

Because of the wonderful quality of the drawing, the chief of police ordered that no one be placed in Cell 8 again.

On August 20, 1967, the section of wall that contains the work was cut out, framed, and enclosed in a protective glass case.

Today this drawing hangs on permanent display in the main lobby of the police academy in St. Louis. Every policeman and new police recruit sees it every time he or she enters the building.

For over seventy years now, the legend of Cell 8 has attracted thousands of schoolchildren, church groups, artists, writers, and ex-cons from near and far to gaze at it.

More than he could possibly imagine, the work of this unknown and downcast artist has endured as a silent and powerful testimony to the power of faith.

The Author

Then Jesus cried again with a loud voice and breathed his last....Now when the centurion and those with him, who were keeping watch over Jesus, saw the earthquake and what took place, they were terrified and said, "Truly this man was God's son."
(Matthew 27:50, 54)

11.

I Helped Him, Now He Helps Me

I am a prison chaplain. Have been for many years.

I ministered to one man in particular, I remember. The Lord changed his life. He got released, and several years later he became the pastor of the church where I attend every Sunday.

So you see, I was his chaplain, now he's my chaplain.

G.M.

"For the Son of Man came not to be served but to serve, and to give his life a ransom for many."
(Mark 10:45)

12.

Be with Me in Paradise

1:00 a.m.

January 28, 1949

Dearest parents and brothers, so close to my heart, these lines I am writing are the last you will receive from your son and brother.

I am writing them more with my heart than my pen…

I am in the condemned cell, and only a few hours remain before I leave this life.

After my life of ill luck…God has granted me the extraordinary grace of enabling me to recognize my past faults and of making my peace with Him. He has given me this opportunity for a sincere confession, which has opened, little by little, the gates of heaven.

It only remains for me to ask your pardon for all the heartaches I gave you during my life, with my straying—and to recommend to my brothers, whom I love with all my heart, never to stray from the path of duty which you, my parents, taught us to follow with your good advice. I never remembered you with such affection as at this moment…

The end of my career has arrived. Praise be to God, who gave me these moments to ransom my life, and to die as do those men who have faith.

If you want news of my last moments, write to our chaplain, J.R. He will tell you about the last hours spent by me in this world. Be sure I am going to heaven to pray for you, my dearest parents and brothers.

Signed by my own hand. My last thoughts on Earth are with you. Adios! 'Til eternity, your son and brother awaits you in heaven.

(This young man held a crucifix in his hand during his execution, which led Eduardo Bonnin to launch the Cursillo movement, now known as Kairos, a phenomenally successful prison ministry that reduces recidivism from 90 percent to 15 percent among inmates who participate.)

T.S.

Then [the thief] said, "Jesus, remember me when
you come into your kingdom." Jesus replied,
"Truly I tell you, today you will be
with me in Paradise."
(Luke 23:42)

13.

A Weapon to Resist Temptation

My name is G.G., I'm twenty-eight, and I've been strung out on drugs since I was fifteen. Now I'm in prison and I'm getting my head clear for the first time. I look in the mirror and I don't even recognize me. I look like hell.

So last night I went to this Bible group and they read about Jesus being led into the desert and tempted by the devil. I see that's what happened to me. The devil tempted me. I gave in so many times. I sold myself out to Satan.

One guy in the Bible group said we're all tempted, just like Jesus, and we can look to Jesus as an example of how to resist temptation, and that if we pray to Jesus, He will help us to succeed just like He did. I said, God, that's what I need, real bad.

We all prayed out loud for help, me for drugs, one guy for smoking, one guy for stealing, one guy for drinking, and all kinds of things. We talked about how Jesus answered the devil the same way each of the three times He was tempted. Jesus quoted the Bible, used the words of His father God like a weapon.

We talked about how Satan wanted to tempt Jesus to "bow down and worship him," but Jesus said, "Only my father shall you worship, Him alone."

I've been worshipping drugs. I've called drugs my best friend. But drugs are my worst enemy. That's why they call the devil the "Prince of Lies."

I pray every day now and every night for you, Jesus, to take away my desire for drugs. I want to love you, Jesus, more than I love drugs. I liked the end [of the temptation story], after Jesus resisted the devil: "The devil went away and angels came and ministered to him."

That's what I want, Jesus. I want the devil to go away and angels to come and minister to me.

G.G.

Then the devil left Him, and suddenly
angels came and waited on Him.
(Matthew 4:11)

14.

I Had to Lose It All

Dear Friend,

I greet you in the name of Our Sovereign Lord, who has blessed us with all spiritual blessings. We have arrived at this wonderful season once again, wherein our Savior Jesus is lifted up high and glorified, even to the uttermost parts of the earth. Truly He is the "reason for the season."

Since I came to the knowledge of truth, which God has given to all who believe, I have discovered the true essence of what "Christmas" is all about. He wants us, created in His image, to imitate His son Jesus. "For unto us a Child is born, unto us a Son is given." Indeed, God gave us love and light, grace and truth, the fullness of Himself, everything that He is, so that in Him we might be partakers of His divine nature, become one with Him and live eternally. Oh how I thank God for Jesus!

When I was younger (and of the world), Christmas was all about good eating and what kind of gifts would I receive from so and so. As I reflect, I feel compelled to confess that I was a selfish, egotistical individual. Again, thank God for grace and mercy. Oh, and how painful it was for me to give, either of my time or (especially) my finances. While being a proverbial Scrooge toward my family and friends, I spared no expense when it came to giving to myself. How contrary I was to God at that time. For He gave His best to a people who are undeserving, yet He spared no expense.

Ten years ago, according to worldly standards, I was doing quite well for my age. I was in school, owned my own vehicle and townhouse, and had closets full of clothes, jewelry, and literally a girlfriend for every day of the week. I had it going on, and in my head, *I* was the man. However, I was living knee-deep in sin and day by day it was rising higher and higher until I was totally consumed. As the Word says: "A little leaven will leaven the whole lump." It was like a train wreck. Before I knew it, I had lost everything and was sitting in a cell with a thirty-five-year prison sentence. Indeed, it was a sad, sad story. The calamities that fell upon a young man with such potential—God worked it all together for the good. For in my despair, in my loneliest hour, I met the Savior.

I had to lose it all and come to prison to discover what Christmas and life in general are all about. I have learned that it profits a man absolutely nothing to gain the world, for he is in danger of losing his soul. What I have now in Jesus is far greater than any worldly possession that I had or hoped to have. In Him I am satisfied and content. More important, day by day my desire to emulate Him and be the man that He wants me to be increases. Thus, He is faithful to His Word, which says: "He that has begun a good work in me will perform it, even until the day of Christ," and "It is more blessed to give than to receive."

Why the testimony? I felt it necessary to share with you a bit of the man that I used to be. The old Darcy would have taken advantage of your good will and, no doubt, I would have abused it. I shared this with my mother and she reminded me that the old Darcy no longer exists.

I realize that God has called me to be His spokesman, and that in my journey to becoming what He wants me to be, He will use brothers like you to help equip me to get there.

Your brother and friend, D.M.

"For those who want to save their life will lose it, and
those who lose their life for my sake will find it."
(Matthew 16:25)

"Do not judge, and you will not be judged; do not condemn, and you will not be condemned. Forgive, and you will be forgiven."

(Luke 6:37)

15.

I Thought They Were All Fools

Dear Friend,

You may remember me. I'm the guy that got in all the trouble over killing those seventeen people. It was all on the TV news.

The chaplain came to visit me here in prison when I first arrived. I said, go away, I didn't want to see him. As he left, he tossed a Bible on my bed and said, "You're going to need this."

I never thought a book could make such a difference in my life or have such an impact on me. I never realized until now that the Bible is no ordinary book and is much more than a book of stories. To me the Bible was just a book that collected dust on my coffee-table or was something that took up space in a desk drawer of a motel room. It's hard to believe that I've never read any part of the Bible until now.

The Lord over the years has tried to enter my life many times, and I never let him. Many people in my life tried to tell me about the Lord's love for mankind, and how he sent His Son to die for us so that we may repent of our sins and have everlasting life. I just thought they were all fools and didn't know what they were talking about. I figured I had everything I needed in life, and I didn't need God in my life.

Well, I guess I'm the fool. In the direction my life was headed, it was only a matter of time before I would destroy myself. In my life the only master I served was money. I had plenty of it. Somehow I convinced myself that everything I needed or wanted could be possible with a lot of money, and with lots of money I would be happy. As I started to read the Bible, I stumbled over Matthew 16:26: "For what is a man profited if he gains the whole world, and loses his own soul?"

For me this verse says it best. In a world of much suffering, all I had done was to add more suffering to it. I know I'm going to be in prison for the rest of my life, but I also know the Lord will be with me. I don't want to be here, but if this was the only way for the Lord to finally get to me, then I know this is where the Lord wants me, for the time being. I truly wish I had picked up the Bible sooner and accepted the Lord as my master. But I'd rather be in prison the rest of my life knowing the Lord than to be a free man not knowing the Lord.

What an empty and miserable life I would have had, not knowing the Lord. At least I can say I entered this world with nothing, and I will leave it with the Lord in my heart.

Sincerely, J.S.

From there you will seek the LORD your God, and you will find him if you search after him with all your heart and soul. (Deuteronomy 4:29)

16.

I Found a New Best Friend

I got sent to prison at the age of twenty-three. I thought my life was over. I did not care about anything. I tried taking my life. I did not want to live anymore. My life was really messed up.

One day in prison I met this other guy. We started talking about changing our lives. He asked me if I believed in God; I said yes. He asked if I had ever been to church; I said no.

He told me I should go with him sometime to the church service; I said, okay, I will go. So I went to church for the very first time in my life, in prison.

At first I was nervous because I did not know anybody. After going a few times I got really excited about going. I saw Jesus was born into sin like everyone, but He was sinless. He was tempted by the devil after being in the desert for forty days, but He did not sin. He was crucified and died for our sins, and He was resurrected. Now He comes to each one of us, to you and me, and offers to forgive our sins. He opens the door for us, and all we have to do is walk through it.

I realized I was wrong in my life and asked God for forgiveness. It was like I found a new best friend in Jesus. For once in my life I felt good about myself, like everything was getting back on track. I got baptized in prison, and I felt reborn again, and it was all because I had put my trust in Jesus. As long as you keep Him in your life, everything will be okay.

E.R.

You have been born anew, not of perishable
but of imperishable seed, through the living
and enduring word of God.
(1 Peter 1:23)

17.

How to Show God's Love

The judge just sentenced me to five years in prison.

I'm not happy about it, but I deserve more. I used to get drunk every night and do stupid things, like stealing cars. Then I met a nun who convinced me I was one of those people who has a real problem with booze. I promised her I would never drink alcohol again. That was eighteen years ago.

My life turned around, and everything was going great. Then I fell off the wagon (jumped off) and the first night of drinking I landed here in jail. Dumb.

While I was waiting for my court date, I lived in a jail dorm with about thirty other men. One night about a month ago, I wrote a Mother's Day card for my mother, and it was stolen. I figured out who stole it and I beat him up.

So for the next two weeks I'm living in the dorm and looking at this guy with his eye all busted up by me. I start to think about how I'm about to go in front of the judge to ask him to forgive me for committing a crime. But here's this other guy in jail I beat up. I'm thinking, how can I ask the judge for forgiveness if I can't forgive this guy?

I'm going to die someday, and I'm going to have to appear before God, and I'm going to have to ask Him for forgiveness, too, for all my sins. So I forgave this guy for stealing my Mother's Day card, and I went to him and asked him to forgive me for beating him up. He didn't have to, but you know what? He forgave me. That made me feel good. He showed me the love of God.

V.S.

> "So when you are offering your gift at the altar, if you
> remember that your brother or sister has something
> against you, leave your gift there before the altar and
> go; first be reconciled to your brother or sister,
> and then come and offer your gift."
> (Matthew 5:23)

18.

Those Who Sin Against Us

My stepfather starting raping me when I was six. I told my mother, and she did nothing to stop it. In a way that was worse. Why would a mother not protect her own daughter? I thought God was punishing me because I was a bad girl. I was so angry and confused. Finally I ran away from home when I was thirteen and went to live with an aunt.

If you know a girl who has suffered this experience, you should know it has changed her, deep down inside, and it will make or break her. She's going to hate herself, and you, and God, and everyone. She's going to hang her head and battle with demons inside herself. You have to love her, be gentle but firm, and pray for her. She's going to need a lot of understanding.

I had nightmares and asked God, why didn't He just kill me? It opened my eyes about the reality of evil in the world. I wanted to kill my stepfather. I knew this was going to make or break me. I asked God to heal me.

One day I read in my Bible: "If you hold anything against anyone, forgive him, so that your Father in heaven may forgive you your sins. But if you do not forgive, neither will your Father who is in heaven forgive your sins" (Mark 11:25–26). This was a hard verse for me to read. Then I realized my wanting to kill my stepfather was a sin against God, and with tears in my eyes I asked God to forgive me, my mother, and my stepfather.

G.G.

"Forgive us our debts,
as we also have forgiven our debtors."
(Matthew 6:12)

19.

I Wanted a Godly Man

My husband and I have been separated for nine years, during which he has been in and out of prison. I had given up on him completely.

Trying to live my life with other men and failing miserably, I spiraled downward with drugs, dragging my three children with me.

Then after a series of events that left me on my knees, I gave my life to Jesus. I started reading the Bible, and every time I read the word *adultery* I would cry. You see, now that I had given my life over to God, I wanted to have a complete godly family. I wanted to be made into a woman that a godly man would want. That was my prayer.

So I found out where my husband was, explained to him that I had accepted Jesus as my Lord and Savior, and proceeded to write him asking for a divorce (new Christian and all, I wasn't aware that God despised divorce). He wrote me back and told me that whatever I decided about the divorce was up to me, but that he had recently made the same decision to follow Christ and wanted to be a part of his children's lives.

We started corresponding back and forth. It didn't take long to figure out that after nine years of separation, it was no coincidence that God had saved us both within a few weeks of each other. God has put love in my heart for my husband and answered my prayer, except only better. He has turned my husband into that godly man. Our God is an awesome God !!!

My favorite passage in the Bible? They all speak to my heart, but I'd have to lean toward Psalm 40, because I was rescued from the mire and now all I want to do is sing praises to

our Lord and Savior. I pray that my testimony encourages others
to turn to Jesus.

In His Name, Amen.

In Him, one more life changed by God

T.D.

I waited patiently for the LORD; *he inclined to me
and heard my cry. He drew me up from the desolate
pit, out of the miry bog, and set my feet upon a rock,
making my steps secure. He put a new song in my
mouth, a song of praise to our God.*
(*Psalm 40:1–3*)

*But Jesus took him by the hand
and lifted him up, and he
was able to stand.*

(Mark 9:27)

20.

If Someone Hurt You, That Was Me

Dear Brothers and Sisters in Christ,

Greetings to all who read this. I pray that at the finish of this letter you, too, will understand how mighty the Lord's love is. Believe me, I have spent thirty years behind these bars, and there was a time that was a do-or-die thing. I did it almost all the hard way...

All my sentences have been for assaults and all due to drugs and alcohol and simply not caring about life....Prison made me a very cold person. It led me to be a part of some of the most violent people in prison. I was here [on earth] to set misery above misery, sent here to take you for all you had, and I do mean to the extreme. Being a hateful and sinful person was my everyday life. I took solitary as a joke; fourteen days in solitary was nothing. I survived by pure meanness and the so-called respect that one earned through fighting....Yeah, prison was me all the way. That's all I knew, and it blended in with what life was on the outside....In all reality I was trash, but the devil had me fooled into thinking I was really something....Now after so many years I see what a fool I really was, a real proud nobody...

Whatever happened to you in life happened because of me. If someone hurt you, I was that person. If someone abused and used you, I was that person. If someone you trusted let you down, that was me....If someone stepped on your respect and love...*that was me!*

Sometimes I wonder why I'm not dead...suicide, yeah, I tried that, too....I think I really knew the devil's ways, and then a few years ago Christians started to show up in my life. I treated some bad, laughed at some. There were countless of them; never did I realize that one planted the seed and others came to water it, the time and patience that took....And then one day I saw a homeboy who went to a program called Kairos; every Saturday as I worked out, there he went....So out of curiosity I applied along with some other hundred and twenty-five men. Surprise, I got picked out. This thing Kairos means a special time for God, which was pretty cool. Food was good till we came to the part of forgiveness—yeah right!...But along with the others I made my list. Boy, the list was long, and then someone said, "Don't forget to put your name down." Hmmm? I never thought of that so I tried it. Then we prayed, and sure I joined in. Then the names were put in a bowl and burnt. And for the first time in my life, I cried. I really cried, for something within me left! Like a heavy guilt, I felt weak and unprotected and felt like running, but somewhere I heard a voice say, "Do not fear my son." That day the Lord came into my life. He broke me down, because for the first time in my life the devil was not allowed to enter me....I've seen so much love from strangers, so much care, so much trust....I accepted the Lord into my life that day, October 6. Yes, I am a baby in Christ...and since I began my walk, the Lord blessed me and allowed for me to be put in a program that houses forty-eight Christian inmates. Here I learn about the Word and when I go to the rec yard, I minister the Word of our Lord and especially work on gang members, for most of them are young and in the group for all the wrong reasons. The Lord has given me the power to walk among the worst of 'em without fear, for where I seek souls is the same place I came from...

I regret my past. I regret not loving God all these years. I could have avoided my walk through hell....I love my Lord, my life is His, His will I'll do and love each moment of it. He paid a dear price for my sins. I can't recall ever having had a friend who would put his life down on the line so that I'd live, and by doing so, the Lord Jesus Christ lives today as He did yesterday and He'll live tomorrow....I thought that being bad made me a man...."Wrong!" A man is he who walks in the light of Christ. It's not an easy walk but one that is everlasting in blessings...

So many good things have come into my life since I met Christ, and they can come to you also. Open your heart and trust Him. Just confess your sins and ease your heart, He truly hears you....We as humans are too weak for our own good, but with Jesus Christ, He'll see you through. He's been there, think about it, remember those close calls in your life? That was Jesus calling...

Your Brother In Christ,
J.V.

Jesus said, "Those who are well have no need of a physician, but those who are sick; I have come to call not the righteousness but sinners."
(Mark 2:17)

21.

I Killed My Wife

I thought I knew God. In 1984, I killed my wife in a fit of rage. I loved her dearly, and I miss her. I thought I had found peace, but no. I just covered a wound. This weekend, I was able to forgive myself, for I have been touched by the hand of God. I have a new peace, a new beginning. Now I can find God, and myself. What a gift!

A.B.

*Moved with pity, Jesus stretched out his hand
and touched him, and said to him,
"I do choose. Be made clean!"
(Mark 1:41)*

22.

If You Can Do This, So Can I

I was a methamphetamine [speed] addict for twenty-two years, used it and sold it, and raised two children in that environment. I was arrested nine times, was finally convicted of eleven felonies, and was sent to a women's prison here in California.

I left my two teenage children on the street with all those people I called my friends. For almost a year my children lived in a motel, with those friends making sure they had their room paid for and that they were eating; then they went to live with my mother. In a sick way I thought I had protected them because I always did my dirty business in a different room from where they were, and they knew if I was in that room, they were not to disturb me. But still they were affected by that lifestyle.

I was a very hard-hearted, calloused, and insensitive woman. My lifestyle had really changed what I had been—a very compassionate, caring, and sensitive young lady.

How did I go wrong? It's all a matter of choices. I've always had a very rebellious spirit. You say, "Don't do that," and I'm like, "I've got to check that out." That was what put me out in left field. I look at it today and I think, "Why did I ever do those things?"

My parents were very devout Christians, very loving, very supportive. I'm from a huggy, kissy, cuddly family. They always said, "Anything you set your mind to, you can do." I went the exact opposite. I had a void and I didn't know how to fill it. It was in my spirit: If they said don't do it, I was going to do it. There are a lot of people like that, like Adam and Eve when God said, "Don't pick that fruit." I don't blame my parents or my circumstances or my friends. I made the choices I made, so God could take what was considered so ugly and such a waste, and make it something beautiful to help others. Through my suffering and my poor choices, others can see that God is able to do anything.

My parents would help me get out of trouble, help me get a place if I was evicted, make sure this bill was paid, or whatever, and always bailed me out. And then one day they said they were not going to do it any more, so I had no more last resort. My mother said she changed her prayers and just said, "Lord, drop her into the pit; just keep her alive." That's where I went, and I had no place else to look but up to Him. I feel that when everything let go of me—God's protection, my parents' protection—that's when I really had to say, "I surrender. I give it all to You."

I look back on my madness and see that He protected me. He sheltered me for so long, and then because of my hard-heartedness, He finally took some of the protection away, but God was really looking after me the whole time.

I was looking at two consecutive two-year sentences, and all I could think about was my children on the street. I didn't want to continue to be the example I had been to them any longer.

I remember being taken to the prison in shackles and thinking, "Oh my God, what have I done with my life? If I don't change my life, this is where I'm going to spend it, the rest of my life, having someone else control my life with keys, talking to me like I was a piece of trash, treating me like a number." I realized I needed to change my lifestyle.

I was so afraid, this hard woman who was so bad, you know, that no one could faze her. I was so frightened as I pulled up in front of the prison. I could hear the barbed wire cracking, and I heard the Lord say, "Don't be afraid. I'm going to go with you. I didn't bring you this far not to be with you."

I still want to cry when I think about it. I had the most incredible sense of peace, and it made my time there very quick and easy. I spent my time working my job as a clerk and just really getting to know the Lord.

Before I got out, I had all these fears. My family hadn't spoken to me in five years. But they came to visit me in prison and said they could see in my eyes that I had changed. So they were willing to help and said, "When you get out, you come home." So here I was, a thirty-six-year-old woman finally coming home.

Today I'm involved in a women's prison ministry called "Welcome Home," which has helped hundreds of women. We've received over $250,000 in funding. We've done newspaper articles, television, everything an ex-con never thought she'd be able to do. I thought I would always be a drug addict, a criminal. I didn't know how to get out of that life. God has changed me and uses me actively today, speaking in the local jails to other women like myself, writing Bible studies for them, seeing women who I was on the streets with. They look at me and say, "Oh my gosh, if you can do this, so can I." I'm active in Kairos, and I travel all over. God has just done miraculous things in my life that eight years ago I would never, ever have believed I could do. He's an incredible God and I am so grateful to Him for the things He has done, so all I do is seek opportunities to continue to do them.

I never, ever thought there would be a time in my life when my children would trust me again. It took them a few years because I had gotten clean before and straightened out my life before, and I would relapse. I never could get beyond a two-year mark, so it took them about four years before they finally said to me, "I am so proud of you, Mom, and look at what you are doing with your life!" I have to remind them that it's not me who is doing it, but it's God who is doing it, and I'm just obedient now. When you are obedient, He gives you such great rewards!

Today my children are still being affected. My daughter is using the same drug that I used, and my son is running from the federal law, but I have a complete faith and trust in God that if He can change my life, then He can do the same for them. He loves them far more than I could ever love them, just like He loves me. If I have to be on my knees like my mother was for me for twenty-two years, then that's where I'll be, asking the Lord to protect them and deliver them from the same life that I was in.

I still struggle after twenty-two years of addiction, but today I know where to go. I don't go to drugs, I go to Him, and He carries me through. Then I walk through those jail doors, and those prison doors remind me every time, because He's given me the opportunity to go back in and see where I could be today if I don't continue to walk with Him and trust Him for my every need.

In a state prison for women, almost eight years ago the old me died, and I now live in Christ.

Praise Him and thank you for allowing me to share with you Christ's unconditional love!

In God's grip and grace,

D.F.

We know that our old self was crucified with him
so that the body of sin might be destroyed,
and we might no longer be enslaved to sin.
(Romans 6:6)

Jesus replied, "Who is my mother, and who are my brothers?"
And pointing to his disciples, he said, "Here are my mother and my brothers! For whoever does the will of my Father in heaven is my brother and sister and mother."

(Matthew 12:48–50)

23.

Lift Up My Head

I was the child in my family who always got in trouble. Started smoking, hung out with the wrong kids, started weed at fourteen, took amphetamines, got pregnant at sixteen. I think I gave my parents all their gray hairs. I knew about God but my faith was minimal.

I met the man I called my husband. I thought he was the one, the man of my dreams, but he wasn't. He was an alcoholic, and he physically abused me almost daily. I left him. I had no finances or place to go, or any money, but I didn't know what to do, so I left my three kids with him. That was devastating to me; I felt a lot of guilt over that.

My life consisted of methamphetamine and alcohol to kill my pain. I was drowning my sorrows, going from place to place, and finally ended up on the streets. I didn't care anymore. For two weeks I slept in the bathroom on the beach. Eventually men would ask me if I needed a room. I'd say yes, but of course I had to do other things to get that room. I didn't think I was doing any prostitution; I was just getting a room, and these men cared. I grew deeper into my drugs and met a guy who said, "You can get paid for doing what you're doing." Then it just spiraled, got so intense, and that's all I lived for, the drugs. I put my life in danger many times, where a gun has been put to my head or in my mouth. I got beat up by a lot of guys. I was jumping in and out of cars with men at two and three o'clock in the morning who I didn't even know. My life was in extreme danger every day. I was looking for love, but I thought I didn't deserve anything better.

There were "Holy Rollers" out there at the time trying to preach to me, and I would just laugh in their face. My whole life depended on getting drugs and getting a place to sleep for the night, and I didn't know which one was more important any-more.

All the police knew me, but there was one officer who would tell me all the time, "You don't belong out on these streets. I'm going to pray for you." I did not think twice about it. Many times I was arrested and went to jail, and would go to the Bible studies just to get out of the dorm. I was not trying to reach out to God, but they were planting seeds, little did I know.

I was in a relationship with a man, and he would literally beat me every day, pick me up and throw me across the room. All my relationships were like that. There was one time where he was choking me to death. I grabbed his hands, and the only prayer I knew was the Our Father, so I just started saying that, and his hands released my neck and he left. It was at that point that I truly believed there has to be a God because He heard that prayer. I don't know how I got that man out of my hotel room but I did. Then I dropped to my knees, and I asked God to take me away from this hell, and I started to cry, because I couldn't live that way any more. I didn't want to be beat anymore, I didn't want those drugs anymore, I wanted to be *safe*. I went right to sleep. That was the last night I ever went on the street.

The next morning I went to court for a pending case and got a year. Now I had a lot of time to think.

We had a man who would come around Fridays and give out Bibles. There was that little mustard seed of faith that was instilled in me as a child, so I reached out for the Bible and just started reading it. I knew there was something in that Bible that I needed to know. I wasn't getting all of it, I was just reading, then I was getting a little bit more out of it, and I became a trustee in the jail dorm. One day I was looking through the plate-glass window at all the other women, and I just started crying and saying "Lord, *help me.*" That's when I truly believe I was born again. Right then the chaplain for the women came through and saw me and asked if I needed prayer. I had never wanted prayer from anybody—I didn't believe in it—and I looked at her and I said, "Yes, I need it now." I know God sent her at that moment. He knew I was ready. The Holy Spirit had me filled, and I broke, I finally broke, and I knew I needed God. I was tired of being in jail, of taking the drugs, of having no one that loved me, and this lady told me that God loved me.

She came every week to see me, to talk and pray. She encouraged me to go to Bible study, so I did, with an open heart this time, with open ears. She told me that she loved me for who I was, and I couldn't understand that, how she could love me, a prisoner, a sinner, in a place like that. It was inconceivable in my mind. She was beautiful, well-dressed, a very affluent woman. She showed me in the Bible where Jesus died on the cross for my sins. I didn't know that, and that was a stepping stone for me. I always had my head down because the drugs I did made me lose my teeth, they rotted out of my face, and because of my shame at who I used to be. By the time I left there, my head was lifted high, and I had tears of joy not sadness. Later she got my teeth fixed for me at her dentist.

She told me that God loved me, no matter what, that He had forgiven me, and that I needed to forgive those people who had offended me. It was a big growing process for me. I had to grow from a baby in Christ, not knowing, not understanding. And I learned from the other women coming in that God loved me. Someone gave me a scripture quotation, Philippians 1:6— "He who began a good work in you will carry it on to completion until the day of Christ Jesus."

When I got out, that's what kept me straight. I went to live thirty miles away from the people, places, and things that got me into jail. Now I'm a leader in a women's prison ministry called "Welcome Home" and "Kairos Outside." I've had a video made of my testimony. I tell them God brought me out of the dangers on the street, put me in a safe place, which was jail, got my attention, and when I was released, He came back out with me.

I no longer rely on drugs, I rely on God. I've been clean seven years, and now I know I'm special in God's eyes. He took something that was so ugly and turned it around to His glory.

God has brought many good people into my life to love me through the hard times. God has restored my sisters to me, my mother, and one of my children, and I now have a grandchild.

Now I'm going to college to be a certified drug and alcohol counselor, and I have an excellent job, too. I'm a supervisor for twenty-five employees. They know who I used to be. I pray for each one of them.

W.M.

You, O LORD, are a shield around me, my glory,
and the one who lifts up my head.
(Psalm 3:3)

And Jesus said,
"Neither do I condemn you.
Go your way, and from now on
do not sin again."

(John 8:11)

24.

God Cleaned Me

As I grew up I attended church, but God was a Sunday Habit, and Sunday only. I sang in the choir and became a member of the young people's group. Life was innocent then. But God wasn't real to me.

When I was ten, my baby brother died from leukemia, and the church I attended was the very church that held my little brother's funeral. How could I worship God there? I became uncertain of the existence of God. God wasn't real to me.

After high school I entered the military, not because I wanted to serve my country, but because I wanted to disappear. I was introduced to many things while in the military, to drugs and addictions. My disrespect for God and my resentment toward him (because of my brother's death) became the grip Satan needed to alter my life. The good I learned to manipulate for bad.

When I returned home, I became a police officer with my best friend from childhood. I did not like myself as a police officer. I had a badge and a gun and a desire to do what I wanted. I was very self-centered, and I had hatred in my heart. I came in constant contact with drugs and the people who used and sold them. I remember that days on patrol I would hide out in a cemetery, the same cemetery where my brother was buried, use drugs, and answer my radio calls. Satan had his hooks in me. We would "set up" drug dealers and bust them, take their merchandise, and let them loose. Satan was my master...hell was awaiting me.

Life changed suddenly one evening when my friend and I smoked a confiscated PCP cigarette [angel dust]. I recall the intense high, the feeling of superiority, but it was to be the darkest day of my life. I passed out, and awakened to witness my best friend lying across a bed, dead from a bullet fired from his very own gun. I remember placing my service revolver to my head and crying out to God. He heard my cries and it is only through His mercy and grace that I'm here today. The very next day I buried my best friend, and with him I buried my police badge. I felt God was saying to me that I had to die also, or live with a perpetual guilt.

The FBI investigated his death because of the drugs and money found in his apartment, and I began my federal prison sentence.

The very first face I encountered was an inmate who asked if I believed in God. We talked and I prayed that day, over and over. While there, I was fairly active in church, but I did not give God my all. Got out, once again went back to drugs, violated my probation, and returned to prison.

While in prison I lost my mother to terminal illness. Satan plagued me with guilt: "Your mother's last days and you aren't with her." I turned to God with a need to understand death. I found strength in my mother's "homecoming"...I can't explain the strength, but only in Jesus was I strong.

I began to realize that I had to search for heavenly things, spiritual things, and to know Jesus as a Savior. I surrendered and gave God all of the hidden secrets and desires I harbored. I gave back to God my *will*.

God cleaned me, washed me, and sealed me with His Holy Spirit. I sing a new song today, and it's because God heard me, saved me, and gave me the gift of grace.

I asked God why...why did I go through hell to find salvation? God through His word told me: I had to be delivered, to become the vessel He uses to deliver.

I've replaced hatred with love, and I'm a new creature.... Old things have passed away!!

C.J.

So if anyone is in Christ, there is a new creation;
everything old has passed away; see,
everything has become new!
(2 Corinthians 5:17)

25.

Let Go and Let God

My life was in such distress because of my son's incarceration I felt that I was ready to be committed to a mental institution. My depression was completely immobilizing to the extent that people were beginning to avoid me.

My friend encouraged me to join Kairos ministries so I did. When I first went with them to a prison weekend, I felt I was among ordinary people. I wondered what I was doing there or what I could possibly have to offer. I began to realize that Kairos women were far from ordinary, to say the least! As they each gave their testimonies, I sat and listened in awe of them. I was amazed at what they had overcome in their lives.

Their stories began to inspire me, and I realized that there was hope for me, too. But most of all I began to see that ordinary people can do extraordinary things to make a difference in this world! Here right before my eyes was living proof that God takes a bad situation and makes goodness come from it, that He makes a way where there seems to be no way. His love cuts right through mountains! He meets you right where you are! I felt His presence so strong in the prison that I just sat there like I was dreaming the whole thing. When I looked outside, there was a beautiful rainbow right over the prison. I knew for sure that He was there. I began to sing to myself, "Let the same spirit that raised Christ from the dead dwell in me—Let it quicken my mortal body." And even though it was uncomfortably warm those four days, I just kept going on. Angels were truly all around us. I knew I was surrounded by women who were beautiful, talented, brave people who had so much potential if given the chance to express it. But most of all they were my most precious sisters in Christ. I knew but for the grace of God I could easily have been one of them.

I began to thank God for all the angels that He had put around my son where he was incarcerated, and I knew that God was working on his life and that I had to "let go and let God." I could no longer "be" in that cell with my son—I had to go on my own journey in life and make my own way back to God. "Nothing can ever separate us from the love of God."

Each time I meet with the Kairos women I feel blessed. They give me the strength to go on. When I go to bed at night, I pray to God to teach me to learn to be quiet and remember to "Listen, listen, love, love" [the Karios motto]. Teach me to live the prayer St. Francis taught us so maybe someday I can stand bravely before my sisters in Christ and give *my* testimony. In the meantime let me be a useful member of the Body of Christ and do all that I can to help.

I've learned to stop dwelling on the past. I've learned to forgive. I've learned how God heals the brokenhearted, how to share everything I have with others, how to count my blessings. My prayer is for God to keep working on me so someday I can look back and remember where I came from and my progress.

Everything isn't "all about me" anymore. It is to be a blessing to others and to thank God every day that I'm free and can play a part in helping people to know the Lord Jesus!

My son tells me that he is proud of me. He has done beautiful artwork from his prison cell so I can give copies to the ladies I visit. I praise God every day that something good is coming of my son's incarceration. He has gotten his high school diploma, teaches art in prison, and has written several books. When I went there for his graduation, his teachers told me he is a natural-born teacher and in inspiration to the other inmates. He tells me he expresses his love for God through his artwork.

With love, peace & joy, N.H.

In all these things we are more than conquerors through him who loved us. For I am convinced that neither death, nor life, nor angels, nor rulers, nor things present, nor things to come, nor powers, nor height, nor depth, nor anything else in all creation, will be able to separate us from the love of God in Christ Jesus our Lord.
(Romans 8:37–39)

26.

God Restored My Joy

I do have a story, and it begins ten years ago. I had been imprisoned by bitterness, hatred, and unforgiveness far longer than I had actually been in prison.

The temptation of free food (food brought from outside the prison) was enough to get me to go through a weekend ordeal of Christian fellowship. But I found a love there that I had never experienced as a child or any other time in my life. I had known nothing but abuse in every way. Heck, it was why I was there; after all, I had killed my stepfather. I even knew of God, but not personally enough to think He still loved me after all I had done. (I have to say, since my grandfather was a deacon at a church and I watched him molest girls for years, I did have my confusion about church folks, too.) As overwhelming as the whole weekend was, I wish I could say that I changed overnight, but I didn't. A few things stuck in my heart like glue though, and Psalm 51 was one of them. Besides all this love that seemed to be too good to be true, a lady shared her testimony and used this psalm in her talk. It didn't take long for me to figure this David and I had a lot in common. No one knew I secretly kept reading the psalm, hoping God could create a clean heart and renew a right spirit in me, but wait a minute—restoring the joy of His salvation meant I already had it.

I had accepted that Jesus died on the cross for me as a child, but was taught about not wearing pants or cutting my hair, not how I had to trust God with all the pain in my life, let alone take responsibility for forgiving those who hurt me.

I thought these ladies must have nothing else to do but come visit us for this weekend, but they kept coming. And when I didn't show up for reunions, they asked about me and wrote to see how I was. Well, the letters sent to me through the years really told the tale. They encouraged me with the Word. It had to be real, but since I didn't know what was real at this point in my life, I wasn't ready to trust yet. However, no one gave up on me.

So one day I asked the Lord to do for me what I couldn't do for myself, never knowing He would turn me every which way but loose. It was the beginning of moving past existing in life, to surviving in prison, to actually living life. I was paroled to a Christian halfway house for women who had been incarcerated; then I got the opportunity to go back to visit prison to minister as part of that women's team. Yes, it was quite an eye opener. This side of the fence was different. I'll never forget being overwhelmed as I had to return to a place I thought I would never step foot into again. God had answered my prayer and given me a clean heart and a right spirit, and He surely has restored the *joy* of his salvation. Now I didn't want to leave and had to grow past the emotions of knowing how they felt and hurt so. The experience—the honor of being able to give back what was given to me—overwhelms me every time I get to work as a team. This year marks the ten-year mark. There are so many experiences from the first to the last, but I hope that this brings hope to the hopeless and shouts loud that God loves us right where we are at and that He will do the changing!

C.S.

Create in me a clean heart, O God, and put a
new and right spirit within me...then I will
teach transgressors your ways.
(Psalm 51:10, 13)

27.

Journey's End

There I sat, January 21st, in the city justice center, with a charge of aggravated murder.

On this particular day I was trying to kick a heroin habit (cold turkey). Withdrawal from the dope had me sick as a dog. My sickness had me balled up in knots, with sweat all over my body; my teeth chattered and I stunk from the dope coming out of my pores. All I could think about was escaping from my agonizing aches and pain. I had hit rock bottom with my drug addiction. I had reached the apex of my insanity; now I was being introduced to a threshold of excruciating pain I would never forget. I was too sick to concentrate on my murder charge. All I could think about was getting some relief for my agonizing muscles and bones.

It was during this time I met a young man named Carl, who used to walk around the cellblock witnessing to the men about the love of Jesus and the saving grace of God. For the past twenty-six years I had claimed Islam as my religion of choice, so I really wasn't trying to hear anything about Christianity or any other faith. However, that did not discourage Carl from witnessing to me. One day while I was still withdrawing, Carl walked over to me and started talking. I wanted to brush him off at first, but I knew he meant well, so I listened. When he started talking about Jesus and being "born again," I interrupted and told him, "I am a Muslim on a journey, just passing through this life as we know it."

He looked me straight in the eyes and said, "We are all on a journey. The question is: What is going to be the end of our journey, eternal damnation or eternal salvation?" His question hit me like a straight right hand. I couldn't weave, bob, backpedal, or run. I had to face that question like a man and be honest with myself. There I stood defenseless, dumbfounded with the obvious answer starting me right in the face. My reasoning at that moment was crystal clear: I had just taken a man's life and as far as I was concerned, the end of the journey was going to be eternal damnation. There was no way I could fake myself into believing I had eternal salvation to look forward to. As a result of my sin-tainted lifestyle, I felt I had made it to the major leagues, the point of no return. Carl told me, "Nothing could take away my sins, nothing but the blood of Jesus." I was ready for whatever I had coming, be it the death penalty, life without parole; nothing mattered to me. I hated what I had become and where my addiction had led me. I had a beautiful wife, two wonderful children, a nice home, and a family that loved me. All it took was an episode of my getting high and an argument for me to lose everything I valued in life.

I stood there thinking about these things as Carl talked. I told myself, "If you denounce Islam and convert to Christianity, Allah is going to strike you dead for putting another God before Him." Then I reasoned, "If I should drop dead, I wouldn't have to spend the rest of my life in prison, but on the other hand, if this Jesus is real, I'll have assurance of life after death." I didn't have anything to lose, so I stepped out on my faith, asked for-giveness for my sins right there on the spot, and made a decision to accept Christ Jesus as my Lord and Savior. I've been testify-ing about Jesus Christ and His saving grace ever since that day sixteen and a half years ago. It is said, "A journey of a thousand miles begins with the first step." I took a step of faith, and God allowed me to enter into a relationship with Him and to take a journey, which leads to eternal salvation. I praise God daily for freeing me from my prison of ignorance. Today I realize when you are serving your created purpose, your created purpose will serve you. My question is: What purpose are you serving, and what will be the end of your journey? Serve your created purpose and you will be blessed with joy unspeakable; all it takes is your first step of faith.

D.P.

"The LORD your God has blessed you in all your undertakings; he knows your going through this great wilderness. These forty years the LORD your God has been with you; you have lacked nothing."
(Deuteronomy 2:7)

I learned to love the Gospels in prison as I never loved them before.

—Benedict Groeschel

28.

Is This God or What?

I have, or so I'm told, a very powerful and strong witness.

I was born in New York to loving and wonderful Jewish parents. Many years later I became a very successful businessman with homes in Florida and New York. I had it all! Financial freedom along with the "lifestyle of the rich and famous." My world collapsed when I got into a fight with my wife's ex-husband. I was found guilty of second-degree murder and got life in prison. That was twenty-one long years ago.

My three-piece suit was exchanged for "blues." The custom Italian shoes, cars, houses, and business are all gone.

My wife and I divorced. She was ten years younger than I was, and after losing one appeal after another, I sent her on a new path and life. We kissed goodbye, said we loved each other and always will—end of story!

We exchanged cards, letters, and such over the years, and I gave her my blessings on a new marriage. I felt it best for our daughter.

Eight years later she came to visit me and told me of the profound change in her life—she and our daughter both gave their life to Christ. I told her she was crazy, she's Jewish!

"So was Jesus," she said. They asked if they could send me a Bible—I said no and would not give up my life of reading *Playboy* and smoking for some useless faith! My daughter looked at me with those beautiful eyes and said, "Please."

As I did with everything in life, I attacked it with the passion and zeal in which I ran my corporation. Ever the skeptic, I fought it for eighteen months. How could I as a Jew accept a new religion? I looked for any critical tenet to doubt this Jewish Carpenter. There were no lightning bolts! No angelic messengers! I just gave in to the truth! I saw no way around it! The rest, as they say, is history.

When I first gave my life to the Jewish Messiah, Yeshua, I met with a young rabbi who was also a believer. I remember asking him, "What do I do now? Go to church or temple?" I'll never forget what he said: "Go where God leads you and be with good Christians." I asked, "How do I know who the good Christians are?" Again he said, "They are the ones who love Jesus and Israel."

Over the past twelve years I've received a degree in biblical history in addition to my independent studies in Christian apologetics. As I'm working toward another degree, my thesis will concern the problems facing the "Jew" of today. I've written a small booklet called "The Promise," which was inspired by my walk. If I know nothing else, I know the mind of a Jewish person. If you can get the Jewish person to believe in a God who created everything from man to thermodynamics, then why not the resurrection? After all, the resurrection is the "key" to the Christian faith!

In the meantime, I'm studying and learning as much as I can. I've read the Bible cover to cover every other year and still I know nothing!

Where the journey will take me, I can't say. I don't feel a calling to preach or prison ministry. My heart is with the young (I love kids) and the Jewish people. I've set mini-goals but there are still only twenty four hours in a day. It's been said, "Only a fool learns from his mistakes, when he could have learned from someone else's!" And so I'm looking and learning. I feel very blessed to have come this far and enjoy the love, health, and peace that come with a relationship with the Jewish Messiah.

Something profound is happening in my life and I know the hand of God is on it. With my kind of sentence, I'm not supposed to leave here alive. Yet three months ago I was called into classification and told I was being dropped to minimum custody and sent to forestry! Recently I was again told the parole board will see me. I'm being considered! Is this God or what? Twenty-one years and soon I may be free.

I ask that you pray for me. Not for parole or freedom, but for God's direction and His will in the life of this Jewish boy from the Bronx! In the meantime, may your lives continue to prosper!

Shalom! In His Name, G.S

I am not ashamed of the gospel;
it is the power of God for salvation
to everyone who has faith.
(Romans 1:16)

"I tell you, there will be more joy in heaven over one sinner who repents than over ninety-nine righteous persons who need no repentance."

(Luke 15:7)

29.

For the First Time in My Life

My name is C.V. I'm forty five-years-old, and for the first time in my life I live in a blessed state of joy and peace. God has truly poured His grace and joy into my life.

I've been in and out of prisons for thirty years, always on dope charges. I've lived such a hard drug life, high stakes and plenty of action. I've overdosed three times and was in a coma for two months. God pulled me out of this hell. I always thought there had to be a God, but I wasn't buying no air mail baby Jesus stuff. I would read my Bible and see scripture like, "I am the way, the truth, and the life. He who believes in me will have eternal life." How could I overlook scripture like that? And then I saw "If ye have faith as a mustard seed..." So I put this mustard seed faith into action, and I would pray through Christ, and I did truly seek to know Him.

Then one day I was watching some preacher on TV and the Holy Spirit came over me. I'll never forget that wonderful feeling I experienced that day, that washing by regeneration. My morals changed and my spirituality changed. I was cleansed in the blood as I stood there with tears rolling down my face. What a wonderful thing I was experiencing! "It is no longer I who live, but Christ who lives within me. If any one be in Christ, he is a new creation." Man, I get so excited when I think about all the wonderful things that God has done in my life these past three years! That joy and contentment that comes from walking in the Spirit. I know when I walk in love, peace, joy, long-suffering, kindness, and patience, it's not me but Christ who lives within me who is manifesting Himself through me. I have become an instrument of God.

Just because we are new creatures doesn't mean that we are not going to have problems. This joy that I have doesn't always mean I'm happy. Happy is by chance, joy is by the grace of God. Romans 5 tells us to glory in our tribulation: tribulation produces perseverance, perseverance produces patience, and patience produces character. God will help us through these valleys that we go through. He will protect us with His rod and staff. Sometimes God allows us to get ourselves into these situations so that we will be still and know that He is God.

I'd like to close with a poem:

This here is a story about a young man's death behind bars
And in his heart before he died laid some mighty deep scars.

Now this young man had been guided by the power of darkness all
his life
With Satan using dope as his weapon, cutting through him like a
knife.

It was sad to watch this young man as he gave up all hope
For now in Satan's eyes, you could see, he finally beat him with
his dope.

But right before this young man died, I heard him reach within
and say
Lord, please forgive me for I have sinned this final day.

I've never seen a man give up hope and die this way
But little did I know of the blessings he'd receive this glorious
day.

As I stared this young man in the eyes, first the left and then the
right,
There was no more darkness, now they were filled with light.

The light began to pour out of his eyes and into his face.
Right before my eyes a miracle was taking place.

Now it was obvious there was something gone but it wasn't he,
For he said, "I can do all things through Christ who strengthens
   me."

I've never seen hatred change into love, so much love,
As the young man dropped to his knees and prayed to his Father
   above.

This is a true story from a prison cell.
I know, for I am the one in this story I tell.

Sincerely, D.W.

"Be still, and know that I am God. "
(Psalm 46:10)

30.

My Past Does Not Dictate
My Future

My name is L.L. and I just want to fill you in on what God
brought me through. I pray that what I say can change the life
of someone who might be struggling in life today.

When I came to prison, I was very bitter, angry, and truly
lost. I thought I had everything but yet I had nothing. I was
trapped in a world of sin and didn't know who I could talk to,

who would understand my hurts, pain, fears, and tears, yet I lived each day as it came.

I found myself still running from life's disappointments, even in prison, being more lonely than ever, and putting my trust in man when I should have turned to God, the Creator of all things, who knows me better than anyone.

I began to ask God to help me and make me whole, because I didn't want to be who I used to be and experience any more struggles that would lead me astray. I wanted something new, and God heard my crying out to Him, that I had truly had enough. He started doing for me what I could not do for myself. I felt the presence of God, and it was then I knew He was with me, guiding me and walking with me every step of the way. I no longer run from my past and what I've been through, because I am with God today. I know that my past does not dictate my future, therefore I've let it go. I no longer keep alive things that should be released. No matter what it is, it does not matter if people judge me or persecute me. I know I have been delivered because He's my deliverer. I don't have to get defensive because He's my defense. And in the strength of Jesus, I can stand and not give up.

I'm not happy I came to prison but I am grateful for getting closer to Jesus, and finding out what He really means to me. I am a new creature in Him, the old things are passed away, behold all things are new. I thank God prison saved me, and I hope my testimony will save someone else. Give God a chance. He will come through with a blessing for you. He did for me.

K.K.

So if anyone is in Christ, there is a new creation:
everything old has passed away; see,
everything has become new!
(2 Corinthians 5:17)

31.

Locked Up Don't Mean Locked Out

I am a fifty seven-year-old woman, and I grew up in the city. My father was a pastor from Mississippi, my mother was a drinker. I came from a broken home, four brothers and two sisters. My mother gave me away when I was two years old to her older sister. She and her husband had good jobs and I had everything a black child could want for. Now after the years passed by, I began to grow up a beautiful young lady, going to church every chance I got. I was sixteen years old when I had my child, who I gave to my aunt and uncle and then I moved on, with a life I thought was good.

I started out with the street life. For many years I walked the street making money, but that was not enough. I went to jail for two years, I came out, but I chose to steal again, and I found myself back in jail. I got out again and did something worse than stealing. I almost killed my man over some drugs. Back in prison—I still had learned nothing from that. In a few years I was back in again for four years for robbery. I thought many times about giving my life and will over to God, which I did. But as soon as the door was open, it was back to the races again. I wasn't home any time before I was back in jail. I just want to say how often I cried out for God to take away my drugs and my stealing.

I have found God now, sitting here in my cell. I gave my life over to Him as much as I understand Him. He gave me so much. I look back on my life; I could have been dead. But God saved me from death. I didn't realize how bad I had become, being an eight-time loser. But now I can truly say, I am a nine-time winner, because I have been made alive in Christ. Yes, my life was to end because of my sins, but because of God's love for me—He is rich in mercy—He made me alive again. I have hope now. I have faith that I can do all things, through Christ who strengthens me. It's okay today. I have peace, joy, happiness, and I am very content within myself.

I have a new life in Christ Jesus, who paid a price for my sins. I am grateful to know that if I leave tonight, I'll be with Christ in heaven. I know I am a conqueror, because all things work together for those who love Him, who have been called according to His purpose. God gave me a choice. I have a new life, to go out and tell young people how He saved me. I don't know what's going to happen in court, but being locked up don't mean that I am locked out. Praise God.

C.K.

*So you also must consider yourselves dead to sin
and alive to God in Christ Jesus.*
(Romans 6:11)

*"The thief comes only to steal
and kill and destroy.
I came that they may have life,
and have it abundantly."*

(John 10:10)

32.

I Was Headed to Destruction

I'm not too good at writing, but I wanted the people who will read your book to know just how great our God is and what He has done in my life through His Son, Jesus Christ.

I was lost in the world of drugs; I had been getting stoned since I was about ten years old. I was working so many hours and used cocaine to keep me up when I was down. I didn't have hardly any free time and met women for sex sometimes on my lunch hour. One night, I couldn't sleep and saw a pastor on the TV from Mississippi. So I watched him. I cried to God, feeling helpless and lost in my sinful world. I felt like I was on a merry-go-round and couldn't get off. I was headed down a road to destruction, using more and more drugs. I got far behind on my car note and was paying my dad to live with him. With what I had left over, I'd buy drugs. Then my dad kicked me out of his house. I went to stay in a trailer with a friend.

Right when I thought things could not get any worse, I was arrested at two in the morning. They said they found pornography at my dad's house and that it was mine. They also said I was in a photo raping my niece. You couldn't see the man or the little girl—I can tell you it was not me raping my niece. It was all on TV and I was sick about it. My mom and stepdad stuck by me, but they sent me to prison with a life sentence plus forty years. I felt the world was against me, but it didn't matter now.

I know that Jesus is going to come through. He is with me through all this. If I hadn't come to prison, I would have overdosed on drugs or got shot and killed. I am so happy inside now, and I have learned not to depend on where I am to make me feel at peace, but to let the peace of Jesus give me rest. And not to let external things govern my joy and peace—but to let Jesus rule in my life. He gives me a peace that surpasses all understanding.

My dad sold the house and moved out of state, and I've never heard from my sister or niece. But the joy I have from Jesus keeps me going, and even though they all think I'm a person who raped a little child, I don't even care what they think or say. As long as I know the truth and Jesus is Lord in my life, I can face tomorrow because He lives. I know He does and He is my strength. One day, I will be out of here. I know He's going to provide a way. I'm going to tell everyone about how my God worked in my life to save me from death. Just keep your eyes upon Jesus and not on the waves of the storm, and you'll walk out to Jesus on that water. He'll take your hand and calm the storm.

J.L.

"They reeled and staggered like drunkards,
and were at their wits' end. Then they cried to the
LORD in their trouble, and he brought them out
from their distress; he made the storm be still,
and the waves of the sea were hushed."
(Psalm 107:27–29)

33.

From Masks to Miracles

God is the God of second chance. He never gives up on us. Even if we fall, He is there to pick us up, dust us off, and help us move forward. No matter how hard we fall, it is never too late to find the forgiving grace of our Savior, Jesus Christ.

I am a living testimony of that. Eight years ago, I fell to the very pits of despair. The pain inside began to eat me alive. Hooked on psych meds, morbidly obese, and in complete denial, I simply existed from day to day.

Growing up in a dysfunctional, abusive home, I found solace in reading. I knew and memorized the Bible. When in my teens I began to suffer emotional breakdowns and repeated suicide attempts, those verses echoed in my head, thus keeping me from falling into permanent insanity.

As a young adult, I sought love and attention. With no self esteem and little value to myself, I found and perfected the art of wearing masks. Those masks kept people from seeing the pain that lay so deep within. The masks were hiding the real me.

I fell in love, so I thought, and married a man who I knew would take all my problems away. Yet he had his own baggage and pain. The breakdowns, addiction to psych meds, attempted suicides, and eating myself into oblivion continued. I hid in the pews of church, attempted to portray mother and wife—all the while the inside of me rotted away.

Then I began to show signs of the point of no return. My cries for help only received pats on the back with assurances that it would be okay. I clung to people who did not know how and were unable to help, when I should have cried out to God.

Finally, one day I erupted. Everything I knew, everything I had, was gone in a split second. I went too far. And because of it, a life was lost. I killed someone. The damage was done. I lost my husband to divorce and my son to adoption.

That was eight years ago. But the story does not end there. In fact, it is just the beginning. Jesus took my mess and gave me a message! For God is truly a God of a second chance. For since my arrest, I found the true meaning of life. It is one thing to know Jesus. It's another thing to know Him personally and intimately.

I found that He can and is able to bring us out of our mess and turn us around. It does not happen overnight, but it is a process.

Jesus forgave me. He loved me so much on that cross two thousand years ago, He took the condemnation of my crime and bore it for me so that I could find true life and freedom in His Name. He paid the price for my crime so that I do not have to live in guilt, shame, and pain. He forgave me. He saved me.

As I have come to abide in Christ and accept His mercy, grace, and love, He has brought me into a closer, more intimate walk with Him. He has shown me there is a reason for living. There is soundness of mind. There is eternal life through accepting Him as my Savior and Lord.

He has taken a wretched mess undone and torn off the masks, healed the pain within, and given her a life of hope and purpose. At first I had given up. I let the prison doctors dope me up. I gave up on my appearance and hygiene. I ate myself up to three-hundred pounds. Still He loved me enough to meet me where I was at. Somewhere along the way, I turned to the God of my youth and He took me in. He gave me hope and purpose. He gave me a new life.

Since then He has begun to restore me. He healed my mind. After twenty years of psych meds, I quit. Jesus gave me His mind—the mind of Christ.

Then He began to chip away at the weight. In a period of two years, I lost 150 pounds. He gave me a song to sing, a word to speak, and a life to live. He gave me a support system of people who look past my crime and see that I am someone who is worth loving. I have found a joy and a peace in knowing Jesus in a deep and personal way. I have found self-esteem in Christ, value in who I am in Him, and love for others and myself.

I cannot undo what Satan did to me—and I cannot bring back the life I took—but Jesus on the cross gave me a future of promise, purpose, and potential. He allows me to walk in the knowledge I am forgiven of killing someone and am free inside.

Truly, Jesus set me free. And he who the Son sets free is free indeed! No longer do I seek a way to hide under a mask, but instead I seek the One who gave me life. Though I still have time to do, I know I do not do the time alone.

C.S.

He will transform the body of our humiliation that it may be conformed to the body of his glory.
(Philippians 3:21)

"Indeed, God did not send the Son into the world to condemn the world, but in order that the world might be saved…"

(John 3:17)

34.

In This Cell I Am Free

There are many types of prisons. We have the prison we grew up in, which is carried with us. There is the world we live in that is a prison in itself if you fall into one of its many paths of temptation. That journey is where I found myself praying for the infilling of the Holy Spirit. What I am trying to say is that I have been locked up all my life in one type of existence or another.

My name is L.K. If you were to meet me, you would be surprised. I look like the most conservative, prim, proper lady. And that I am since my drugging days are over. This is the last skeleton in my closet, and I will begin my life as the Christian I was raised to be. I grew up in the affluent suburbs. My mother was a devout Catholic, and my father was a very passive, hard-working provider. In fourteen years of Catholic education I learned the Bible inside and out—so I thought.

My first prison was at home; my oldest brother had a mental disturbance, and I was fat and was teased at school about both things. I prayed to God to help me many times. He helped me to endure the daily teasing and the outburst within my family. Then my mother died and this shattered my faith in God. So began my travel on the paths of self-destruction—alcohol, drugs, the quest for love. I led two lives—the one you saw in pain, and the one in secret where I felt love and acceptance—I was a substance abuser in every way. My pain needed a quick fix and I found it. Eventually my drug use was a prayer to God to let me die and get out of this life I was in. Even with all the sin, making it by faking it—God kept me alive.

It all came to a head, and I found myself in jail on a felony facing one to three years' imprisonment. On the outside I left my thirteen-year-old son and mentally disturbed brother. Both had very strong beliefs in God. My brother prayed for me daily at church all those years and to this day. My son trusted the Lord would guide me out of my addictions. Their prayers were answered and I was blessed with five years of drug and alcohol sobriety. One addiction at a time was healed.

God blessed me with a good man in my life—who loves me in spite of all that is wrong with me. Yet inside my faith was not strong. You see, many times I prayed in times of trouble, bargained with God; but I never committed myself to him. Then the other shoe dropped, so to speak, and an old piece of my past came back to haunt me. An old case for theft I was involved in years ago was brought up, and I was arrested at my job—in my straightened-out life. Then it seemed the world was ending.

When people look at me here in jail, I stand out. No one would imagine me as a drug user or criminal. In the middle of all the confusion, I started going to church services in jail. One of the other women had a joy about her; she was filled with the Holy Spirit. She was a comfort to me and an example of sisterly love.

This time of atonement has given me the privilege of looking over forty years of my life. Finally I can look into my Bible and take time to study it now. I have searched my soul and see where I went wrong before and where temptation leads me even today. In this cell I am free—at peace within myself. Jesus truly died for my salvation. All I do in my life now will be for the Lord Jesus Christ. Forgive yourself and forgive others who are baggage in your past. Take your sins and throw them in the ocean. Accept life's short-comings. Be grateful to God for His tireless love. God is with you no matter what. Sometimes we don't know it. Each day I pray for the Holy Spirit to fill me. Finally I have a plan for my life—I am on the right path and ready to do what the Word asks us to do.

L.K.

Your word is a lamp to my feet and a light to my path.
(Psalm 119:105)

35.

I've Been Redeemed

I would love to share what Christ has done in my life, especially if it would help others who struggle with drugs, addictions, and crime.

I'd been incarcerated for twelve years—the first eleven years doing things "my way"—when Christ reached out to touch me last year. He alone completely transformed my life. It was nothing but the unfailing love and grace of God that I've been redeemed in order to praise Him and share His mercy with others.

I pray that God's grace and mercy will be with you always, that He continues to bless you and reveal his truths to you.

In Christ's love, H.

Let the same mind be in you that was in Christ Jesus.
(Philippians 2:5)

36.

I Thought Christians Were Weak

My parents love and fear the Lord greatly and raised me according to the Word of God. I went to a Christian elementary school and was homeschooled for middle school. During that time I started to perceive Christianity as weakness and rebelled.

For the next two years I got worse. I was hanging out with some not so good people and started using drugs and alcohol.

Got kicked out of two different schools. Ran away about a dozen times and got in trouble with the law. Finally I ran out of the state, broke juvenile sentencing, and just did not go home. I stayed wherever I could, constantly high or drunk. Things got worse and I was broke. I couldn't go home or I would be arrested. So I robbed for money again. This time I was identified. A week later I was caught. In jail on armed robbery and burglary with a deadly weapon, I wondered where my life was going. Having just turned sixteen, I thought I could make it on my own. I found out I can't.

It was then I realized who my friends really are. Mom and Dad came to see me every week. They were who really cared for me, not my partying friends. I turned my life over to the Lord and He has healed many broken relationships. He took my drug and alcohol problem and gave me a new "high" through the Holy Spirit. No amount of drugs or alcohol could ever make me feel the awesome joy I now have in Christ Jesus.

Since then I've really got to know Jesus. He has brought me through so many difficult times and continues to daily. I've read through the New Testament nearly four times and each time I get new insight and better understanding of God and how He wants me to live.

I planned to buy and do so much when I got out of here, but now I realize that the more I buy and do, the less time I will have to spend with Christ. It didn't burst my bubble, just put my priorities in right order.

I've met a lot of true believers here, who show the love of Christ and inspire me to earnestly seek that unfailing, *agape* love. God is so good. I now try to bring others to that realization. I've had some of the best times of my life, strangely enough, in prison.

Love in Christ, N.S.

For he was crucified in weakness,
but lives by the power of God.
(2 Corinthians 13:4)

37.

Spiritual Warfare

I entered into a spiritual warfare on the day I was born.

Satan, our enemy, attempts to defeat us with strategy and deceit, through well-laid plans and deliberate deception.

I come from a broken family. My mother and father divorced when I was four years old. My oldest sister ran away from home around this time at the age of fourteen. I was bounced around from home to home, mother, father, and grandparents. Just as I would settle in, meet new friends, and get acquainted in school, I would move someplace else. Satan created this instability to use as his advantage. As I became a teenager, I became withdrawn, insecure, hopeless, angry, rebellious, and lonely. My father was an alcoholic. He was not physically abusive, but he was verbally abusive. My mother was addicted to pills, such as pain-killers and muscle relaxers.

I started doing marijuana at the age of nine. By thirteen, I was taking pills and experimenting with other ways of getting "high." I ran away from home when I was fifteen. By then I was doing acid, smoking pot, drinking beer, taking pills, and eating [hallucinogenic] mushrooms. By the time I was eighteen years old, I had started snorting cocaine. I got involved in a life of crime. I was burglarizing homes and businesses, dealing in stolen property, dealing in drugs, committing fraud and so, so much more.

I got arrested and sent to prison. I left behind a lovely wife and a two-week-old son. After getting out, it didn't take me long to fall back into my old ways. I had the mind concept of "I want what I want when I want it." Anything I wanted was mine.

I was arrested and sent to prison again. This time my wife was tired of the way I was living and wanted a divorce. When I got out of prison, I could see how I had hurt my wife and two sons. I had caused a loving family to fall apart. I felt the pain deep inside but continued to go about my devastating ways.

One month after my divorce I married another girl. That lasted exactly two years. Again I was arrested and sent to prison. Upon my release I thought about changing my ways. That is about as far as it went, a "thought." I was out for a year, arrested again, and sent to prison for a fourth time. I couldn't believe it. Only this time I wasn't looking to get out of prison—I was to spend the rest of my life here.

I looked back on my years and saw all the people I had hurt. All the destruction I had caused. I started to cry because I hated the way I had lived my life and how it was turning out. I thought about suicide.

As I lay in my cell thinking one day, I felt the Holy Spirit comfort me with this warm feeling, telling me everything was going to be all right. I had lived a life of pain and misery, but that was about to change. I reflected back on a certain day. It was my 21st birthday and I was in prison for my first time. On that day, I had gotten baptized and I asked Jesus to come into my life. I felt God talking to me as I lay there in my cell. He told me that if I had let Him be in control, my life wouldn't be the way that it was. So I prayed for God to take control of my life, to help me get out of this vicious cycle I had gotten myself caught in.

God has come into my life and He has changed me in ways that would take a lifetime to explain. He has brought love and joy into me. A different kind of love and joy. I thought hanging out at parties, getting high, and sleeping with girls was "love and joy." But it wasn't. That is only a deception of Satan himself. I thought money was the answer to my problems. But it wasn't. I hurt and had a lonely feeling inside the more money I obtained. I have no money now and I feel better than ever. God has introduced me to people who love me for who I am, and not for what I have. God has shown me how to battle Satan's desires and temptations through the Word of God (Bible), through fellowship and prayer.

God has taught me patience, love and kindness, joy and peacefulness. I can see clearly now my future, living as a son of God. I no longer live in that dark day-for-day living. Praise God!! There are no more thoughts of loneliness and despair. God is always there. Please allow Jesus to come into your life as He has mine. God bless you !!

E.C.

Put on the whole armor of God, so that you may be able to stand against the wiles of the devil. For our struggle is not against enemies of blood and flesh, but against the rulers, against the authorities, against the cosmic powers of this present darkness, against the spiritual forces of evil in the heavenly places.
(Ephesians 6:11–12)

*Jesus looked upward and said,
"Father, I thank you for having
heard me. I knew that you
always hear me."*

(John 11:41)

38.

I Was Blind But Now I See

My name is C.S. I'm thirty-three-years old and I have four children. I've been incarcerated for the last one and half years. I don't want to be a drug addict or alcoholic anymore. My addictions led me to crime.

I tried everything in my life except God. Then I prayed for God to change my life and change me. Last year God spoke to me, and this time I was obedient to what He said. He said to quit smoking cigarettes. I've been smoking cigarettes for over twenty years! At first I was kind of hesitant about what God said, then my nose started to burn and I haven't smoked a cigarette since—thanks be to God!

I've been blessed throughout my life because God saw fit for me to be on this Earth. But since I've accepted Christ as the head of my life and as my personal savior, change started to take place in me and in my life. Once I was blind, but now I can see. Once I was lost, now I'm found. I was deaf, but now I can hear! I've also been blessed with a talent that I didn't know that I had—writing poetry (see following page).

God's love is so precious and caring. Even though things aren't the way I want them to be at this moment, I'm better than I used to be—and through the grace of God and His loving mercy He has given me a new attitude about myself and life. I thank God for allowing me to do His will and not mine.

C.S.

"Your kingdom come. Your will be done,
on earth as it is in heaven."
(Matthew 6:10)

Remember Me

Remember Me
　　I was so pretty & sweet
　　How did I end up on the street?
　　Sometimes I didn't eat or even sleep
Remember Me
　　So tall and strong
　　How did I end up doing wrong?
　　Now I sit here all alone
Remember Me
　　As a child
　　Wondering how I became so wild?
Remember Me
　　When I cried out loud
　　My voice was heard throughout the crowd
Remember Me
　　When I had sinned
　　God has given me my life to live again!

Stop and Listen

"Stop and listen," a voice said in my head
　　While lying down in my bed.
　　It softly whispered, "Peace, be still,
　　and let God do His will."
"Repent and turn from your sins.
　　I will give you a new life to live again."
　　God has blessed me with that special ear
　　Letting me know He is always near.
Stop and listen.
　　"Remember when I raised Lazarus from the dead?
　　And the little girl from her deathbed?
　　They too heard a voice whisper in their head."
Stop and always listen
　　Or you will miss your blessing.
　　"That battle is not yours," the voice said.

That's why God's only begotten Son is dead.
He paid the price for our sin.
Repent in order to win.
Please stop and listen.
You'll never know when that voice will come.
When it does, please let God's will be done.

C.S.

39.

I Want Answers

I want answers to questions now. I want to be enlightened at the moment something is going on, not at a later time like a suspense movie with a surprise ending. I don't like being kept in the dark.

Let's take this place, for instance. I know I'm here to be punished. In response to prayer my sentence wasn't as harsh as it could have been. With some difficulty I'm slowly accepting this. But what's the real reason behind the reason? What's God up to? I could have been a candidate for alternative sentencing, but I wasn't. I could have gotten away when I ran, but I didn't. When I ended up at the beginning of the circle, I knew God was controlling everything. I distinctly know it. So why does He want me here? Whose life am I supposed to influence or contribute to? What is my function? He won't tell me and He offers no clues. That's the frustrating part. What am I supposed to do? I thought I was to get involved with this church, but that wasn't it. You know when God is opening doors for you. I thought I had a future in sheet metal; no go. I feel like I'm going through an instruction course, just before you are given your assignments. The avenue to Bible school was closed. The road to increased academic skills was closed. Not blocked, but completely closed. I kind of got the impression God wanted me to focus more on Him and less on the things *I thought* He might want me to do.

But see, that's just the problem. I'm running from Him. I have no idea what He wants me to do and I'm too scared to *really* know what He may ask of me. Sometimes He can ask for a lot, more than I think I might be willing to give. Something is for sure. When it came to teaching, I put my foot down. No way, no how. I tried it once, and it got too complicated.

Another thing is service in prison. I'm terrified that part of His plan includes serving Him for ten years as an inmate and not a volunteer. I wouldn't want that either. So I go down my list of things I think God wants me to do, hoping this might be one of them. But sooner or later I'll come to the end of my list. And He'll be there waiting. And the funny thing is that when I do find out, it could be one of the easiest things He could have asked of me. Something that I would have enjoyed.

So my difficult area is simply trusting Him. I'm confident He knows what He's doing, but I'm so scared He may ask me to serve Him for some umpteen years in a prison. That's not the future I want. But with whatever time I have, I hope to learn all He's placing before me so that when the time is right, I'll be ready because He says I finally am.

Some day I hope to be like the angels that simply obey God's word...He speaks and they go. It would be easy to trust Him then.

E.D.

I will trust, and will not be afraid, for the LORD
God is my strength and my might;
he has become my salvation.
(Isaiah 12:2)

40.

Prison Taught Me

This period of incarceration has taught me a tremendous amount about humbleness and humility.

More importantly, it brought me closer to the Lord. I read the Bible and pray every day. I'm going to keep doing this when I get out. One of the things I'm planning to do when I get released is to return to school to pursue my degree in business. I'm also planning to volunteer for some local community service project through my church. Thanks for your prayers.

Peace and Christ be with you always, R.

The reward for humility and fear of the LORD
is riches and honor and life.
(Proverbs 22:4)

41.

Blessed Life, Not Cursed

Grace and peace be to you. I pray that all is well with you in all aspects of your life.

I'm blessed of the Lord and things are getting better and better every day. The Lord is truly good to me. I'm just steady walking with the Lord trying to take advantage of every day. I'm truly looking forward to that day I'm released. I'm ready to start over, walking in the new path of my life.

I truly want to do what God wants me to do. I want to be used by Him. I want to live the blessed life and not the cursed life. I'm so grateful for revelation knowledge of the Word of God. It has revolutionized my thought life. I just bless the Lord, for He is good.

I pray that you be blessed with strength and joy always.

Love, S.M.

I call heaven and earth to witness against you today
that I have set before you life and death, blessings
and curses. Choose life so that you and
your descendants may live...
(Deuteronomy 30:19)

42.

I Have Already Received

I totally gave my everything to Him. I have poured myself out, and been filled with the true Spirit of God. This I am still learning to do daily. I pray, Lord, please live *your* life through my life, and help me divest myself of me.

O, how I praise God. I was for so long praying amiss, until my friend and teacher opened my eyes to the truth about having already received all that God had for me! This spiritual understanding started overflowing my spirit.

At this point I knew that I needed to spend time alone with God. So I started in prayer, read my daily devotions, four to be exact. Then I settled in on my bed, with ear plugs, and closed my eyes. I called on the Lord, stirring up the spirit, letting Him know I was here for this blessing, now. I just started praying, praising God, and deep within me I felt a surge of power and emotion. I opened my mouth, started crying and praying in unknown tongues. The tears turned to joy, then more tears. What a joy and spiritual blessing I was enjoying.

God has truly shown me what obedience is about. You must claim your place in His kingdom. I keep saying, "And God shall get the glory from my life." And many people have come to tell me that they see God shining through in my life, time after time. Believe me when I say, this is Jesus Christ living in me, and not me. I give all the glory to God. I try and pray in the Spirit daily. I never want to lose ground that has been taken from Satan.

Your brother and friend, K.

*Through the law I died to the law, so that I might live
to God. I have been crucified with Christ; and it is no
longer I who live, but it is Christ who lives in me.
And the life I now live in the flesh I live by faith
in the Son of God, who loved me
and gave himself for me.*
(Galatians 2:19–20)

43.

Heaven on Earth

May grace and peace fill you through our Lord and Savior Jesus Christ. The Father's seed has grown so much in me that I am always talking and praying with the Spirit. I can see my natural life here on Earth becoming more like heaven on Earth!

Things I used to like (when I was unsaved) I don't even desire, and I can't see how I ever did those things. I can't even understand how I lived without the Holy Spirit in me.

In the seed of Jesus that is in me, is the potential to be more like Jesus as long as I apply myself. I just want people to see Jesus when they see me. Now I can look forward to being more and more like Jesus.

Your brother in Christ, D.C.

*"Be perfect, therefore, as your
heavenly Father is perfect."
(Matthew 5:48)*

*Jesus said, "Go; let it be done
for you according to your faith."
And the servant was healed
in that hour.*

(Matthew 8:13)

44.

Lack of Knowledge Has Been My Downfall

I realize that lack of knowledge of truth is the cause of my backsliding and the reason why I'm in prison today.

I want to know Jesus. And the only way for me to do that is through His Word. I also know that I need to know His Word in order to be able to stand on His Word when the enemy attacks. Lack of knowledge has been my downfall. The only way for me to be sure that I'll never fall like that again is to know the Word of God and to apply it to my life—or apply my life to it!

I need to quit leaning on my own understanding. I will be diligent in my studies of His Word, and allow God to give me wisdom.

L.

"Very truly, I tell you, anyone who hears my word
and believes him who sent me has eternal life,
and does not come under judgment,
but has passed from death to life."
(John 5:24)

45.

It Doesn't Feel Like Prison Anymore

The Bible is my "desert place" where I can come and rest.

I got saved two years ago—too late to keep from coming here but in time to bring Jesus with me. Over the months here my heart began to harden, but Jesus has been a rejuvenation for me. It doesn't feel like prison anymore! It'll never feel like prison again.

I accepted Christ two years ago in prison, and then I was on fire for the Lord and He took over my life. I shared the Word with my brothers, but then I turned my back on the Lord and I was miserable for a long time. But this weekend has brought Jesus back into my life! I'm scared though and want you brothers to help me and pray for me. You've taught me a helluva lesson.

What I like about our Bible study here in prison is that the room is filled with black and white guys but it doesn't matter— there is just love here, a whole lot of love. I've been in prison eighteen years and this is the first time I've ever hugged another human being, let alone a man. It feels good, and I know those hugs are hugs of love.

S.P.

*I have loved you with an everlasting love; therefore I
have continued my faithfulness to you.
Jeremiah 31:3*

46.

When I Get Out, I'm Going Right Back In

I've spent most of my life since I was thirteen behind bars. Since I found Christ, I've been looking for a new direction for my life.

With your prayers and help, I've decided to go into prison ministry. When I get out, I'm going to walk right back in again with the Lord.

B.B.

"I have given you as a covenant to the people,
a light to the nations, to open the eyes that are blind,
to bring out the prisoners from the dungeon,
from the prison those who sit in darkness."
(Isaiah 42:6–7)

47.

I Quit

To: Satan and His Demons
From: K.T.

Subject: Resignation

Please be advised that I resign as your servant and chief
protégé as of September 13. You are a *liar* and the father of
deceit. You no longer have control over me. I quit!!!

I have accepted a new position with the "life assurance
firm" of Jesus Christ!!! The benefits are pure joy, eternal love, life
beyond compare, never being alone, lots of hugs, and never feeling "filthy" on the inside. My new boss, my Lord and Savior
Jesus Christ, washed me in His own blood. I'll serve Him until
He's ready to take me home.

So long, Satan—and be aware that I *will* tell *everyone* what
a liar you are. I'll do everything in my power to love them to Jesus
Christ. His policies are free!! Paid in full!!

Signed,
"The New" K.T.

Jesus said to him, "Away with you, Satan!
for it is written, '
Worship the Lord your God,
and serve only him.'" (Matthew 4:10)

48.

I Found Love

I found a way to forgive. I have not cried in nine years. My mother did not love me, and I last saw her when I was thirteen. I had no self-love, no compassion. I came to prison confused; I didn't know what to expect.

But on Saturday night at the church service, I found hope, a better understanding of *agape* love. I was amazed at the love and support from those who do not know me. I am overwhelmed. This can only be the love of God. I forgave my Mom.

S.C.

Then the LORD said, "I do forgive,
just as you have asked."
(Numbers 14:20)

Forgive your people who have sinned against you, and all their transgressions that they have committed against you; and grant them compassion in the sight of their captors, so that they may have compassion on them.

(1 Kings 8:50)

49.

I Found Power and Love

There is a guy in the pod [the prison unit] who I have problems with. He met me at the door, mad at me, accusing me of being a Holy Roller. I said, "Here, have a bag of cookies." He was stunned.

"What are these for?"

"Because God loves you and so do I, brother."

"What does it cost?"

"Nothing, it's God's love."

It hit him again. He turned and walked away with his cookies.

I heard later he was talking downstairs about the Christian upstairs. I went down to tell him not to talk bad about me.

Later, I heard him talking again, saying, "That dude, he's OK."

B.G.

For God did not give us a spirit of cowardice,
but rather a spirit of power and of love
and of self-discipline.
Do not be ashamed, then, of the testimony about
our Lord or of me his prisoner, but join with me in
suffering for the gospel, relying on the power
of God, who saved us and called us with a
holy calling, not according to our own works
but according to his own purpose and grace.
(2 Timothy 1:7–9)

But God proves his love for us in that while we still were sinners Christ died for us.

(Romans 5:8)

50.

I Was Hard-Core

I was one of those hard-core cons, mired and deeply rooted in that pit of sin. I had attended several churches in my early years, and I always felt unwanted, unaccepted. So I rejected any attempts of Christian fellowship. My hurt and pain became hardness and bitterness. I was destroying myself.

Then, out curiosity, I accepted an invitation to attend a Kairos weekend, sure I would find another group of self-righteous, egomaniacal Christians that came here to pound our sins deeper into our minds, and send us all off to hell if we didn't repent!

Today I am a new creature in Jesus Christ! For the first time in my forty-five years of existence I met "God's Church," His people, and they loved me, hugged me, loved me, hugged me, and loved me and hugged me some more. Not once did they preach or condemn—they simply loved me to Jesus....

I have served eighteen-and-a-half years in prison, and of all the programs available (and I have been through them all), only one changes lives... Kairos, and the love they give through Jesus.

How does one even begin to express the words "Thank You" to someone who has saved your life—or to the hundreds who gave of themselves physically, mentally, spiritually, and emotionally to lift one out of the pit of death and destruction?

I say "Thank You" by letting my light shine and by loving my fellow "cons" as you have loved me. By allowing others to *see* God's perfect will in my new life and my walk with my Lord and Savior, Jesus Christ!

L.T.

We love because he first loved us.
(1 John 4:19)

51.

Bring Me an Ax

I read a story about a pastor named Joseph Parker who went to hear the great pianist Paderewski (1860-1941) at a London concert.

Pastor Parker, who was also an accomplished musician, was so moved by what he heard at the performance that he did a strange thing when he returned home. Standing by his piano, Parker called to his wife, "Bring me an ax."

Today in church service I heard great music for the first time—the real Word of God. By comparison, what I can do amounts to nothing at all. I feel like chopping my piano to pieces.

Parker did not follow through, of course, but he realized that he could never be a Paderewski by simply following his example. He would need Paderewski's hands and, yes, the very soul of the great musician.

Now as followers of Christ, we know that we can never live up to the "performance" of the Lord Jesus, our Great Example. We might even feel like giving up in despair. But because Christ lives in us, we have what we need to keep growing toward spiritual maturity and Christ-likeness.

Oh, yes, Christ is our pattern, but thank God, He is more. He is also our power. Praise God! Pass this letter along please, if you can.

In Christ's Love,

S.

For the LORD takes pleasure in His people;
He adorns the humble with victory.
(Psalm 149:4)

52.

Better Off in Prison

As soon as I got here, I was put in a cell with a guy from Nigeria.

I was a lost soul, angry at myself and the whole world. This guy starts talking with me about eternal life, and I tell him to shut up.

Little by little he taught me that I have value and that I am valuable. He said the God who created the universe also created me and loves me. He showed me how easy it is to pick up the Bible and just start reading.

One day he was free, and he walked out of the prison and was run over by a car. Right in front of the jail! It was a terrible accident. The newspaper the next day had this headline: "He Was Better Off in Prison."

I'll always remember him in my prayers, all the things that he said and did for me. I thank him for his compassion, understanding, generosity, kindness, acceptance, encouragement, and so many other things. He enriched my life and restored my faith, hope, and love for humanity.

M.J.

Faith, hope, and love abide, these three;
and the greatest of these is love.
(1 Corinthians 13:13)

*There is therefore now
no condemnation for those
who are in Christ Jesus.*

(Romans 8:1)

53.

I Was Not Lost But Found

My name is K. I am thirty-eight, no kids. I pray when I get out I will still be blessed with the ability to have them. The majority of my "life-changing" experiences have happened here in jail. My origins are from a wealthy suburb full of "high moral ground." I am the youngest of six children in a nonpracticing Catholic family. When I was six years old, the family business was going under, and my father left my mother without any cash, home equity, or job experience. In order to take care of us all, she stepped up to the plate, and went to work.

My stepfather came into my life when I was seven. When he knelt down with open arms, I remember praying, "God, please don't let him leave us like Dad. I promise to be the best little girl ever." From that point on, my character-building began. I carried my cross of abandonment, emotional, verbal, and now sexual abuse from my stepfather.

Does God put anything in our lives we can't handle? Since then, without success I used drugs, alcohol, anger, blame, and every excuse possible. I married, then after six years, divorced. At age thirty-three I began a new chapter in my life...*jail*.

I spent the first three months in jail talking every Wednesday with a true "child of the King," a deacon named E. He and I spoke about God and faith. I questioned God's love for me, and whether I had any faith at all. He said, "Look at the markers in your Bible, that shows faith." I realized God's purpose for my time in jail; I was to use it to go backward and begin the long process of healing and forgiving. To hug that little seven-year-old girl, from the inside. It was at our fusion of hearts, young with old, that I first felt God's meaning of unconditional love. I learned I could do the impossible, and with a higher level of faith and trust, moved forward into complete understanding of forgiving others.

To forgive as a true follower in and of Christ means that I need not forget but only pray that I no longer allow any negative attitudes associated with those behaviors to penetrate my being. Additionally and equally important is to pray for anyone who has hurt us, that they too can find comfort in God's love and forgiveness. For them I pray. Quite simply the key is to "Let go and let God." After all those years of wanting to, I could and did.

Then without warning my ex-husband (a professional sports player) came to visit me in jail. He declared his love for me still. My white knight had arrived. My awakening hit me deep in my soul, that "God put me through all this—just for this moment." The overwhelming unconditional love I felt from God brought me to my knees in prayer. I wish I could now tell you "The End" or that I lived happily ever after. No, not even close. We did not get back together. He met and married someone else. No matter, for I was not lost but found. The feeling that God shared with me that day has never left.

Last year I was released, but the devil of addiction called my name and once again I fell, a devastating choice that landed me back in jail this year, *again*.

God's grace fell upon me once again, when one of his living angels opened my eyes and helped me see that God has His reasons and I need not question them. I have a purpose! A destiny! It's the choices I make that decide the path. But first I must learn to totally surrender—mind, body, and soul. God, please give me love through Your eyes, allowing me Your way of seeing love instead of my human way. Help me to love You, God, myself and my neighbor. God is the inventor of love. For His mercy I pray. I've learned to listen to the God inside of me. "He who is in you in greater than he who is in the world" (1 John 4:4).

In my nine-year sentence now I remember the saying from St. John Vianney: "We have nothing of our own but our own will;

it is the only thing that God has so placed in our power that we can make an offering of it."

For me the message is clear…God loves us all, addicts and criminals alike. His love now sings in my heart. I may be losing time in this world, but it will prove to serve me better in the next. I have less fear and more pure joy. I thank all God's people who carry His message. This is my story. Whether you use it or not, it helped me "see who I am." For that alone, thank you. I do not fear tomorrow for God is already there.

J.C.

After you have suffered for a little while,
the God of all grace, who has called you to his
eternal glory in Christ, will himself restore,
support, strengthen, and establish you.
(1 Peter 5:10)

54.

I've Been Transformed

Hello, my friend!

I've been reflecting on my own rebirth. Recalling what I was like and the manner of life I was living. It's hard for me now to accept that I was once so blind, lost, and full of so much sin. It was no wonder that I felt so unworthy and had no hope. Thank God for His Son Jesus Christ and for the Holy Spirit and for the Word of God that doesn't change and is for anyone who chooses to believe. I say this with strong conviction in my heart, because I see how Jesus is calling the lost and tormented without respect to who they are, or what they've done. He offers sustenance to the body and soul while pointing the way to shelter that is ever-lasting.

Yes, I can see this and much more now, since having been transformed into a child of God. I've come a long way on my journey with Christ and know there is still a longer road ahead. I've learned that I'll never be lost or alone again and that there is a purpose for everything. I may not know what each purpose is, because how can I or any person think like God, but I do know that whatever the circumstances, everything and everyone has value in the eyes of our Father.

Truly the Lord has and continues to bless me by having changed me completely, instilled within me hope that is eternal, and opened my eyes, heart, and mind to life. Guiding and protecting me so my life is joyful and fulfilling. Presenting me with brothers and sisters who care about me. Acting upon that love through prayers, words of encouragement, and a constant willingness to point the way to Christ.

As I think of all this on a regular basis, it becomes no task but a joy to write or speak of my walk with Christ. Sharing my growth as a Christian with others helps to lift up the Lord, brings me closer to Him, while taking my faith to a higher level. Praise God!

It does my heart good to hear and learn of others who are doing for the Lord. For the Lord has given and continues to do for us and all of this world so much that we can never repay the price He paid. To give Him praises of glory and honor with humble obedience seems so little in comparison to what He has given and promises to give us.

I hope this letter is able to inspire and strengthen you in your service and walk with our Lord and Savior. I thank God every day for His grace and blessings, giving me the opportunity and the ability to exalt His name by testimony and doing my best to walk in faith without waiver.

Once again I've failed to curb my enthusiasm when writing of the Lord, especially when speaking of what He has done for me (big smile)!

Your Friend,

V.K.G.

The disciples began to praise God joyfully with a loud voice for all the deeds of power that they had seen, saying, "Blessed is the king who comes in the name of the Lord!"
(Luke 19:37–38)

55.

I Am at Peace with Myself

Greetings to you, my brother/sister in Christ. I hope that whoever you are, this story will touch your heart and make you think.

Without this prison sentence I would have lost the battle of life and would never have known His grace and mercy. Yes, I'm truly blessed, and as hard as it may be for my fellow prisoners to believe, I'm grateful to be in here because I was saved by prison!

I am forty-six, a husband, and proud father of two children. By God's grace I am able to give my testimony of my undaunted faith and how prison saved me. My dad was a house painter, like his dad, and like many painters, an alcoholic. Naturally, I grew up to be just like my father, a painter and alcoholic. I could never seem to leave it alone.

I'm here to testify that, looking back over the years, Jesus was there in my life even though I was hell-bent on destroying everything I touched. I was on the road to drinking my life away, just as my parents and older brother did. Now I look back and see where He was in my life, when I was in all those bar fights that turned into the kind of fights where everybody got involved, with knives and guns pulled, or the numerous car accidents that should have killed me.

I survived because He had a plan for me. He never gave up on me. He kept trying to reach out and pick me up and show me a real life, but I was in denial and kept up the party life, drinking and smoking weed, being a rebel, and living a hard life. I think back to the times when I could have turned away from it all and lived life right, but I let the devil use me. I remember so well all the times God would be there, holding out His hand, offering me to get in and take hold. Instead, I just stood beside Him until the smoke cleared enough to sober up, and I did it all over again.

I came to prison at the ripe old age of seventeen, with a three-year sentence. I got out and then went right back in for another three years. Got out again, met my wife, and married her. That kept me out of trouble for ten years until my third DWI [driving while intoxicated] sent me back to prison for five more years. Got released, and went right back to my alcoholic lifestyle.

I knew not to go back to my old stomping grounds where I grew up, but I was pulled back like a magnet to socialize with my old friends and to talk about my older brother, who drank himself to death there. I got into a confrontation with another alcoholic. I hit him in the head with a wood two-by-four. He died from that one blow. I live with regret of that and what I put his family through every day.

In steps my Savior. Time to grow up. Like I said earlier, I was a rebel without a cause, the tough guy image on the outside. Inside I was scared to death, lonely and in desperate need of His mercy. I had allowed the alcohol and weed to cloud my sight; my eyes were closed. I was arrested two weeks later for murder and sentenced to thirty years. If only I could have realized that when God caused me to meet my wife, He was trying to tell me that it was time to stop behaving like a child and be a man, take responsibility for my life and be what He wanted me to be. But no, I decided to run with the devil.

On the tenth of December I decided to be that man. I hit my knees in that cell and asked Jesus to come into my heart to stay. I confessed my sins to Him and asked forgiveness. I placed to rest the old me that night. I know as a sinner I will pay my debt to society for my bad decisions. Now I live my life every day knowing I am living His will. I have been enlightened to all that He has always offered me before. I am at peace with myself.

Now that He is my pilot I know wherever He takes me I will be doing His will and not my own. Where He leads, I will follow. I speak from the depths of my inner soul when I tell you He saved me from myself. Mine eyes have been opened. I have been blessed to have two children who love me and both have been saved and know Jesus. And I am truly blessed beyond my expectations to have a loving wife of twenty-three years now and going strong, who like God refuses to give up on me. She has stuck by my side through it all, bless her heart.

May your heart be filled with compassion for the families of those of us locked up, for they are doing time out there just like we are in here. I've buried the old me, and look forward to being free one day, because I choose life with Christ.

May He fill your heart with joy and mercy as He has mine.
In His mighty name, Amen. P.P.

"Your faith has saved you; go in peace."
(Luke 7:50)

Prayer Section

I Will Trust in the Lord

I will trust in the Lord with all my heart,
And will not lean on or depend upon my own understanding;
I will not rely on my own insight, intelligence, or
What I think I know;
I will trust the Lord with complete confidence!

I will remember and acknowledge the Lord
In everything I do,
And He will reveal and make plain the right way,
And will make my path clear, straight, and smooth;
In the end
He will crown my efforts with success.

I will not be conceited to let myself think
That I am wiser than I am!
I will not be sure of my own wisdom.
I will simply obey God and refuse to do wrong.
I will not think of myself as wise.
Instead I will trust and reverence the Lord
And will turn away and depart from all evil.

(Proverbs 3:5, personalized)

If These Walls Talked

If these walls could actually talk,
Would they tell of my Christian walk?
Or would they just up and say,
That I have gone the wrong way?
I wonder what it would be,

If these walls could tell on me.
Would I come out as shining gold?
Or would I have been left out in the cold?

When things came up that I did not foresee,
Would these walls have told on me?
Would they have said I acted bold?
Or would I wish that it had not been told?

Angry words that I had said,
Would I want to go hide my head?
Or just not want anyone to know
That my bad temper I did show?

Many times the things we've done,
Would not have been a victory won.
Behind these walls things we did,
That we'd rather have kept hid.

By the time each day is through,
What would these walls say to you?
Would you thank God for His grace?
Or would you want to go hide your face?

At the end of each and every day,
If these walls talked, what would they say?

by G.S.

Praise the Lord

Praise the LORD!
Praise the LORD, O my soul!
I will praise the LORD as long as I live;
   I will sing praises to my God all my life long.

Do not put your trust in princes,
   in mortal men, in whom there is no help.
When their breath departs, they return to the earth;
   on that very day their plans perish.

Happy are those whose help is the God of Jacob,
   whose hope is in the LORD their God,
who made heaven and earth,
   the sea, and all that is in them;
who keeps faith forever;
   who executes justice for the oppressed;
   who gives food to the hungry.
The LORD sets the prisoners free;
   the LORD opens the eyes of the blind.
The LORD lifts up those who are bowed down;
   the LORD loves the righteous.
The LORD watches over the strangers;
   he upholds the orphan and the widow,
but the way of the wicked he brings to ruin.

The LORD will reign forever,
your God, O Zion, for all generations.
Praise the LORD!

(Psalm 146)

Amazing Grace

Amazing grace! how sweet the sound
That saved a wretch like me.
I once was lost, but now am found,
Was blind, but now I see.

'Twas grace that taught
My heart to fear,
And grace my fears relieved.
How precious did that grace appear
The hour I first believed!

Through many dangers, toils, and snares
We have already come.
'Twas grace that brought us safe thus far,
And grace will lead us home.

The Lord has promised good to me;
His word my hope secures.
He will my shield and portion be
As long as life endures.

When we've been here ten thousand years,
Bright shining as the sun,
We've no less days to sing God's praise
Than when we've first begun.

Amazing grace! how sweet the sound
That saved a wretch like me.
I once was lost, but now am found,
Was blind, but now I see.

John Newton (1725–1807)

Joseph and the Warden

Joseph's master took him and put him in prison,
the place where the king's prisoners were confined.
But while Joseph was there in the prison,
the LORD was with him;
He showed him kindness and granted him favor
in the eyes of the prison warden.
So the warden put Joseph in charge
of all those held in the prison,
and he was made responsible for all that was done there.
The warden paid no attention to anything under Joseph's care,
because the LORD was with Joseph
and gave him success in whatever he did.

(Genesis 39:20–23, adapted)

The Lord Is My Shepherd

A Psalm of David

The LORD is my shepherd, I shall not want.
  He makes me lie down in green pastures;
he leads me beside still waters;
  he restores my soul.
He leads me in paths of righteousness
  for his name's sake.
Even though I walk through the valley of the shadow of death,
I fear no evil;
for you are with me;
  your rod and your staff—
  they comfort me.

You prepare a table before me
    in the presence of my enemies;
you anoint my head with oil;
    my cup overflows.
Surely goodness and mercy shall follow me
    all the days of my life,
and I shall dwell in the house of the LORD
    my whole life long.

(Psalm 23)

The Beatitudes

When Jesus saw the crowds,
he went up the mountain; and after he sat down,
his disciples came to him.
Then he began to speak, and taught them, saying:

"Blessed are the poor in spirit,
    for theirs is the kingdom of heaven.
Blessed are those who mourn,
    for they will be comforted.
Blessed are the meek,
    for they will inherit the earth.
Blessed are those who hunger and thirst for righteousness,
    for they will be filled.
Blessed are the merciful,
    for they will receive mercy.
Blessed are the pure in heart,
    for they will see God.
Blessed are the peacemakers,
    for they will be called children of God.
Blessed are those who are persecuted for righteousness' sake,
    for theirs is the kingdom of heaven.

Blessed are you when people revile you and persecute you and
utter all kinds of evil against you falsely on my account.

Rejoice and be glad, for your reward is great in heaven,
for in the same way they persecuted the prophets who were
before you."

(Matthew 5:1–12)

Teach Me, Jesus

(An Inmate's Prayer)

Teach me, Jesus, to love all men,
Both friend and enemy; teach me how to wish them well.
Teach me how to be an instrument of Your peace.
Look at my heart...Remove from my heart all
Bitterness and hatred. Fill my heart with a great
love for You, and for my neighbor.

Bless the chaplain, that he will be a light to
Those of us who are in the darkness...A safe
Guide on the path that leads to You.

Bless those who are in charge of this prison and
Those who work here. Help them to do their duties
According to Your holy will...For the physical and
Spiritual well being of all who are confined here.

Bless my fellow prisoners. Help us to see and
Acknowledge all errors we have made in life, and
Help us to return to our Father's house.

Bless those on the Kairos team and their loved ones.
They are angels sent by you to let us know that
There is love outside these prison walls.

Bless our families and all who seek You, Lord.
Keep us, show Your Face to us, and have mercy on us.
Turn Your face
To us and give us Your peace. Amen.

S. D.

Consider It Nothing But Joy

My brothers and sisters, whenever you face trials of any kind, consider it nothing but joy, because you know that the testing of your faith produces endurance; and let endurance have its full effect, so that you may be mature and complete, lacking in nothing.

If any of you is lacking in wisdom, ask God, who gives to all generously and ungrudgingly, and it will be given you. But ask in faith, never doubting, for the one who doubts is like a wave of the sea, driven and tossed by the wind; for the doubter, being double-minded and unstable in every way, must not expect to receive anything from the Lord.

Let the believer who is lowly boast in being raised up, and the rich in being brought low, because the rich will disappear like a flower in the field. For the sun rises with its scorching heat and withers the field; its flower falls, and its beauty perishes. It is the same way with the rich; in the midst of a busy life, they will wither away.

Blessed is anyone who endures temptation. Such a one has stood the test and will receive the crown of life that the Lord has promised to those who love him. No one, when tempted, should say, "I am being tempted by God"; for God cannot be tempted by evil and he himself tempts no one. But one is tempted by one's own desire, being lured and enticed by it; then, when that desire has conceived, it gives birth to sin, and that sin, when it is fully grown, gives birth to death. Do not be deceived, my beloved.

Every generous act of giving, with every perfect gift, is from above, coming down from the Father of lights, with whom there is no variation or shadow due to change. In fulfillment of his own purpose he gave us birth by the word of truth, so that we would become a kind of first fruits of his creatures.

(James 1:2–18)

Make Me a Captive, Lord

Make me a captive, Lord,
And then I shall be free.
Force me to render up my sword,
And I shall conqueror be.
I sink in life's alarms
When by myself I stand;
Imprison me within Thine arms,
And strong shall be my hand.

My heart is weak and poor
Until its master find;
It has no spring of action sure,
It varies with the wind.
It cannot freely move
Till Thou has wrought its chain;
Enslave it with Thy matchless love,
And deathless it shall reign.

My power is faint and low
Till I have learned to serve;
It lacks the needed fire to glow,
It lacks the breeze to nerve.
It cannot drive the world
Until itself be driven;
Its flag can only be unfurled

When Thou shalt breathe from heaven.

My will is not my own
Till Thou hast made it Thine;
If it would reach a monarch's throne,
It must its crown resign.
It only stands unbent
Amid the clashing strife,
When on Thy bosom it has leant,
And found in Thee its life.

George Matheson
(1842–1906)

The Lord's Prayer

"Pray then in this way:

Our Father in heaven,
hallowed be your name.
Your kingdom come.
Your will be done,
on earth as it is in heaven.
Give us this day our daily bread.
And forgive us our debts,
as we also have forgiven our debtors.
And do not bring us to the time of trial,
but rescue us from the evil one.

For if you forgive others their trespasses,
your heavenly Father will also forgive you;
but if you do not forgive others,
neither will your Father forgive your trespasses."

(Matthew 6:9–15)